D1524252

The Art of The Builder

Elevating Construction Surveyors

A Step-by-Step Guide for Remarkable Surveying in Construction

Copyright © 2022 Jason Schroeder
All rights reserved
ISBN: 9798435477559
Imprint: Independently published

Acknowledgements

Jason Lattimore

Jason started in the construction industry in 1994 helping his father in the civil construction industry and has worked in the building construction industry in some capacity or another since 1996. Jason's current role is as Contract Administrators/Procurement Manager for IP Builders, Inc. out of Walterboro, SC. Brandon and I want to thank Jason for all of his professional editing. You were a big help with every section of this book.

Leo Zhang is a Virtual Construction Manager with The Conco Companies in the San Francisco Bay area in California. He focuses on construction technologies including survey/layout, reality capture, and 4D planning/scheduling. He received his master's degree in Construction Management at the University of Florida. Brandon and I would like to thank Leo for his positivity and support as we wrote this book. His comments, recommendations, and additions really helped to complete this work.

Jean-Philippe Simard (J-P) is an application specialist at BuildingPoint Canada where he trains and helps the BuildingPoint Canada customers and team members take advantage of the Trimble Buildings solutions including software and hardware for robotic total stations and laser scanners.

J-P has over 18 years of background experience working with the Cansel Group of Companies in various roles including technical support, sales support, and sales. He has conducted many training sessions and site visits for robotic layout and laser scanning applications. J-P helps concrete formwork companies, steel fabricators and erectors, and MEP companies gain productivity and reduce errors in their daily work by using the hardware solutions of the Trimble Buildings portfolio. You can expect a high level of knowledge and professionalism when collaborating with J-P.

Brandon and I would like to thank J-P for providing on point feedback for this book. J-P gave us some hard things to think about and was able to challenge us on several topics. We appreciate his input and dedication to this book.

Dedication

This book is dedicated to Okland Construction. It is a great privilege in life to encounter other human beings who are dead set on growing and improving with the mindset to bring others along for the journey. Imagine my surprise finding an entire company right in the middle of its decision to reinvent itself every day, never content to rest on past accomplishments or the greatness of yesterday. Thank you for giving me the latitude to be my true self, for allowing me to chase my vision and giving me the platform to aid in the development of others. You men and women leading the way have my everlasting admiration.

-Brandon Montero

Table of Contents

Preface by Jason Schroeder

I spent many formative years with Hensel Phelps Construction Company in a strong culture that included field engineers and intentional survey practices. I spent four years as a field engineer and was then privileged to travel the United States for seven years supporting field operations and teaching field engineers. I can proficiently run AutoCAD, Revit, Tekla, Autodesk Architecture, Sketchup, and Navisworks Manage. I can set up a total station in under 70 seconds and perform any traverse, level loop or layout activity needed in construction. When I was in the game I could operate the total station, automatic level, laser, robotic total station, and GPS units anytime and anywhere. I tell you this only to set the scene for a failure that would come years later when I had an opportunity to run a one hundred million dollar project with a company that did not have field engineers or a relationship with a consistent surveying company. I want to make it clear that I will never run a project in any capacity without those crucial positions again.

I did my absolute best to properly delegate, check work, and organize the survey work performed on my project, and yet we still had a few hundred thousand dollars worth of layout mistakes from misplaced embeds, problems with secondary control, and floors that later needed to be floated. Like many in our industry, I was trying to get $200k worth of layout work done with a $25k budget, and it cost us double what it would have if properly planned. But I have never been a victim of circumstance; I knew better then, and I know better now. Working without field engineers, a trusted surveying company, and the proper surveying practices cost the project money, decreased the level of quality, upset the owner, and prevented people from being home with their families due to rework and overtime.

Each project has the standard questions: what, when, why, how, and where. These are all important, but if you get the "where" wrong, the answers to the rest of the questions may drastically change. The consequences affect not only time, money and other valuable resources, but there is an immeasurable toll that these errors have on business relationships and the morale of the individual, which transcends to their families at home.

I have worked with over 50 different surveyors and survey companies throughout my career. I had never met one that was able to merge the world of field engineering and the world of survey until I met Brandon Montero. He is a true professional. Brandon is the best surveyor and construction surveying professional I have ever met. He understands how to nail a boundary survey and set up secondary control for a building. He knows how to mentor a field survey crew and new field engineers on a construction project. He is the total package and the primary author of this book. He and I have worked together for four years merging these worlds together and have taught hundreds of surveyors, field engineers, and superintendents these practices. If you need to understand the "where" for your project, Brandon is the man that can build the answer.

You may be a professional who brings a wide variety of experience to the table. Brandon and I are not only open to your feedback and input, but we truly invite you to participate in this process. Together, we can help elevate an industry of professionals to higher standards and greater success. As you read this work, please send feedback to:

jasons@elevateconstructionist.com. We look forward to hearing from you!

Until then, enjoy our book. Please rate it highly for us so we can scale it and share it far and wide to help others. Our mission at Elevate Construction is to elevate the lives of everyone in construction. We want to build people up and strengthen families, and we hope this book will do just that. We believe that every training concept understood, every mistake prevented, and every project improved will bring respect back to workers which will ultimately support and protect families. At work we are responsible for supporting, caring for, and keeping safe the loved ones that countless husbands, wives, daughters, and sons loan us on a daily basis. It is our job to be their guardians and champions.

THE ART OF THE BUILDER

Introduction
by Jason Schroeder

I'd like to reference marksmen as a tool to anchor you to the concepts we will discuss. A marksman is a person who is skilled in precision shooting using projectile weapons to shoot at high-value targets at longer-than-usual ranges. The proficiency in precision shooting is known as a shooter's marksmanship which can be used to describe both gunnery and archery. A marksman is highly skilled and revered— much like construction surveyors. Parallels between the two professionals include:

1. Both marksmen and surveyors know their equipment and respect it.

2. They know the rules, regulations and principles that govern application of their capabilities. The marksmen know weapon safety and firing practices. The surveyors know the detailed procedure along with the proper application of mathematics which can include geodetics, coordinate geometry, trigonometry, or survey best practices.

3. They practice relentlessly and both are able to aim and hit small targets. Surveyors are proficient with distance measurement, leveling, total station usage, robotics, GPS, and survey applications.

4. They are skilled in precision. To be a great marksman, there must be precision and calculation in the shot. A surveyor will likewise have a great need for accuracy

to reduce errors and eliminate mistakes in each observation.

5. Marksmen and surveyors can adjust their technique depending on their target. A shooter must be able to hit difficult targets whether under concealment or in the open, and be able to differentiate between weapons based on the desired target and its proximity. Some weapons are slower and more precise while others are characterized by speed with wider, less precise shots, and every combination in between. A surveyor must be able to make accurate shots when needed and faster, less precise shots when production is more important than perfection. There must be an ability to operate seamlessly with either goal at will.

I have a high level of respect for the men and women in this profession. I want to elevate them and the field by doing my best to provide resources and information that will continue the tradition and further promote the role of construction surveyors.

The Survey Commandments

To elevate the individual moving along the survey path, we have assembled a set of commandments. As you read them, you may find that some of the terms are technical or currently outside your experience. Don't worry. As your experience grows, each one of these commandments will take on deeper meaning. Expose yourself to these concepts now, and as you hear key words throughout the course of your career, they will bring to mind these commandments with which you've already become familiar. Additionally, this list may highlight areas in which you're currently able to create additional growth both technically and professionally. When properly implemented, these commandments will ensure that any surveyor can provide a quality product on-site that anyone can use as an accurate and precise reference. The commandments are as follows:

Commandment #1:

Always traverse primary control. Achieve a LEOC less than .02', or "first order" accuracy. Compare Civil coordinates with the traverse coordinates. Analyze X, Y, and Z rotation.

Commandment #2:

Tie back to or verify the basis of bearings (or legal property corners) from the project coordinate system. Verify existing structures (columns, foundation, NOT FASCIA) for proper tie-ins.

Commandment #3:

Always perform a level loop (level circuit) of all primary

control points and include the design/project benchmark in that analysis.

Commandment #4:

All on-site level loops are to be performed by going through two known benchmarks when possible, estimating to the nearest thousandth for rod measurements, using three-wire leveling, and closing the loop back to the start point within acceptable accuracy. Achieve less than .008' or 'first order' accuracy.

Commandment #5:

Horizontal distance measurements are to be done with a total station, tape measure, or a steel chain. No plastic, cloth, or uncalibrated steel tapes are allowed.

Commandment #6:

Always check using a different technology, direction, person, and/or approach.

Commandment #7:

Label everything you lay out and keep good field notes with a pen. Strike through mistakes or corrections, no erasing. I recommend using a waterproof, smudge proof pen.

Commandment #8:

All benchmarks are to be set as a part of a closed level loop and documented. Every building, every floor must have a minimum of two benchmarks to sight and verify while working inside the structure.

Commandment #9:

Establish a baseline with two accurate endpoints. Intermediate points (minimum of two) to be set in-line from the end points as a complete line. Distances should be double verified from each end of the baseline. All baselines are to have a minimum of four points per line.

Commandment #10:

Learn how to use the end of your tape or chain. Always have tape ends in good condition. Measure from zero; never burn a foot.

Commandment #11:

When radial staking, after setting your backsight or performing your resection, always check into a known and established control point before beginning radial layout. Check back into your backsight throughout and at the end of the survey to ensure your angle hasn't drifted.

Commandment #12:

Use a true plumb to calibrate 4'- 0" prism poles. Use mini prisms and a short rod (1'-0" or less) for tolerances less than .01'.

Commandment #13:

Always calibrate your equipment. Work out the frequency with the survey department or an educated vendor.

Commandment #14:

Always plumb vertical buildings from the bottom floor.

Commandment #15:

Always post-process/review field notes and fieldwork the day of to ensure accuracy or catch errors and mistakes before construction.

Commandment #16:

Talk to the person to whom the work order relates; don't leave room for misinterpreting the instruction or detail.

Commandment #17:

When taking notes and recording data, always think about what detail or shots are necessary for someone else to accurately represent your work in CAD.

Commandment #18:

QC and gut check work in the field. Does this look right, does this sound right?

Commandment # 19:

Report issues, errors or mistakes as soon as they are discovered.

Commandment # 20:

Stop and take opportunities to develop your own skill set, or to teach and mentor others.

Survey Principles

by Jason Schroeder

What is a Layout and What is Control?

A layout occurs when you lay out a line, a point, a marker, or an elevation on a construction project to guide the installation of work whether it involves a general installation or the installation of building components.

Control is something that manages all other layouts on the project site. Control is a nice term to use because I like the visual of fist clenching and empowerment. We must control the location and the "where" of everything in construction, and we do that with control points that are more carefully installed and surveyed. Points, as a part of your primary, secondary, or working control networks, must be as close to perfect as possible. They must be protected and networked together with incredible precision and accuracy.

Primary control is permanent, surrounds the project site, and is networked together as a system. This control network is used to control the site. Secondary control is semi-permanent, is building specific, and must be tied to building grid lines. This system is usually built with baselines and controls the layout of a specific building. Working control is temporary, precise, and is used to layout critical building components. Each network helps create the other from primary to working control.

When we transition from the civil site layout such as grading, curb and gutter, or civil structures and utilities to building construction or even vertical construction we will use more and more control networks that are permanent, semi-permanent, and temporary for the work that follows behind.

This is where a surveyor must merge with the world of field engineering. Field engineers and surveyors must partner together to establish a successful primary control network, secondary control network, and working control network that is accurate and precise. This partnership will facilitate layout taken from those networks to build a very precise construction project. If a partnership between field engineers and surveyors is successful, they will not only produce a better product, but the field engineers on-site will be able to successfully use the control networks to guide the layout of the rest of the building, including any vertical components.

Precision and Accuracy

Introduction:

Precision for layout generally means the relative correctness of layout work related to other layout, or to points related to each other in a network. In other words, the geometric correctness of the way points relate to each other is how precision is measured. This dictates that the surveyor perform work in a way which yields a precise product.

Accuracy defines how close points have been laid out to their design or planned position in the real world. In other words, proximity to design location or design coordinates in their correct position within the coordinate system determines accuracy.

Story:

"I remember arriving at a project where the professional surveyor had just laid out primary control. The owner of the project informed us they were ready for us to layout the stick-framed buildings using the provided control as our layout references. There were seven large retirement homes that made up a one hundred and twenty million dollar project that included skilled nursing and assisted living. As a part of the normal practice as a field engineer at Hensel Phelps, I worked with the field engineering team to traverse the points. After doing a basic traverse, closing with an accuracy of over 1:50,000', and analyzing the points, we found many of the points off by hundredths and one was eight tenths off. This network was okay generally from an accuracy standpoint which means it was generally within tolerance in the state plane coordinate system, but it was not precise. These buildings needed to tie together at critical connection points. Had these points not been checked, they would have created continual problems for the construction teams." Jason Schroeder

We must have absolute accuracy and high levels of precision in our survey work.

Application and Challenge:

Surveyors and those performing surveying tasks must have high levels of both accuracy and precision. There are times when accuracy is the main focus and the only requirement because the layout tolerances from point to point are fairly large. This would be true for most civil hardscape, laying out temporary structures, or rough grading tasks. But for most other survey tasks generally, and in construction specifically, we need the points and layout in the correct work location and correct to each other.

In order to accomplish this, the entire industry—which includes surveyors, field engineers, layout foremen, layout technicians, VDC specialists, and superintendents—will want to learn the fundamentals of surveying and construction layout. We will discuss these directly later in the book. Additionally, we need to understand a concept called "false precision." This happens when exact numbers are used for inexact notions. There are several versions of this fallacy—all of which have in common numbers used to give a misleading impression of the confidence one can place in the work. In layperson's terms, a number represented for a coordinate listed to the ten-thousandth does not mean it was surveyed to and accurate to four decimal places.

In conclusion, we must have high levels of both accuracy (real-world location) and precision (relative relationship to other points) to effectively build high quality construction projects on a budget and on time.

Being a professional surveyor or layout technician means we know how to achieve high levels of accuracy and precision. In a later section we will show how following the Surveying Commandments will enable you to do this.

Mistakes and Errors

Introduction:

Mistakes are large and costly deviations from the intended plan or task requirements. Some examples include starting on a building at the wrong location, laying out something only for it to be a foot off, or doing something incorrectly that could have been done correctly or prevented. Errors are typically small and inherent in everything that we do. There are human and instrumental errors in all aspects of surveying. We must understand the difference between mistakes and errors and focus on the elimination of mistakes and then the reduction of errors. We reduce errors by performing our double-checks, doing direct or reverse shots, double-centering, applying forward and back distance shots, and implementing other techniques that help us increase our precision and reduce the inherent error brought by human interaction and in the equipment. We eliminate mistakes by double-checking our work. How often do we find ourselves simply deciding that our level of effort was "good enough" or "close enough" without any true due diligence to back that statement up? By rejecting the idea of "good enough" altogether, we stay on the constant lookout for ways to improve the precisions, speed, and accuracy of our work.

Story:

For example, there was once a time when I was working on a $140 million prison in Victorville, California. It was on that job that I laid out a guard station thirty meters in the wrong direction—which meant that the thirty-meter wide guard station was laid out on the wrong side of two points. Two points were shot in from primary control to provide location of the corners in the building. And I proceeded to lay out the other side of the building on the wrong side of the first two points. This was a large mistake that cost a minimum of $35,000USD. Thankfully, we caught it before we began building the foundations. Only the electrical duct bank had to be moved. It also cost us a lot of time on the project schedule. During the course of the work, I was very focused on making sure that my layout was precise and was very careful to reduce errors. I remember checking the distances from side to side and diagonally multiple times to ensure that I had a very tight network of points for the building itself. I bet that building was as precise a building as anyone could expect, but it was in the wrong location because it was laid out with a massive mistake. As an aside, the electrical superintendent for that company never spoke to me again. If we are to be successful in construction, we will eliminate mistakes, reduce errors, and focus—in that order. What is worse? Having a building thirty meters in the wrong location or a couple of millimeters off from point to point? The answer is obvious. We must first eliminate mistakes and then reduce errors.

We first eliminate mistakes and then reduce errors. Reject "Good enough"!

Application and Challenge:

To apply the challenge, we need to double, triple, and quadruple-check our work. In order to do so, we need to make sure we are using different double-checking methods. By way of application and challenge, we also need to implement the practices for proper construction surveying in order to increase our precision and reduce human and instrumental errors. There is so much more to say in regards to mitigating errors and examples or common mistakes and how they are corrected. Rather than listing them all here, each subsequent section contains examples, stories, and workarounds to drive home this very topic.

The Concept of Double-Checking

Introduction:

This concept is so important it will be approached from a whole different angle in the section "Learn Double-Checks." Double-checking is critical in everything done in both construction surveying and the survey profession in general. Currently, this is somewhat of a lost art in our industry. More often than not, a surveyor will come to the project site, set up on a point, reference a backsight, layout points radially, and perform their work without considering the available and necessary double-checks. When work is done this way, it isn't proven to be either precise or accurate. The right way to do anything if we want to be accurate or precise is for us to double-check our work using the best available methods. We can approach this by assuming a fundamental concept in surveying that everything we do includes some degree of error. We assume that every point, angle, offset and elevation includes either errors, or a mistake of some kind. Always. If we operate under that assumption then we will 100% commit to double-checking and proving the correctness of everything we do.

Story:

I remember a time when I was consulting in Southern California for a large construction company and they were having difficulties with their construction layout and control. The company had experienced elevation busts and buildings had been placed in the wrong location. Problems like these were commonplace. When doing a root cause analysis on this issue, I found the field engineers and surveyors consistently assumed they could do their work properly the first time, and therefore, they were not double-checking their work. Since no system of double-checks was in place, many significant mistakes translated into costly rework over the life of the project. We immediately began to shape a culture throughout the entire company, and specifically in that region, where we assumed everything we did was wrong the first time we did it. This forced people to believe they needed to double-check their work. When that culture started to take root, elevation busts, buildings in the wrong location, and other costly mistakes were reduced and in some areas, completely stopped. This is what we must believe in order to do our work properly.

All layout is wrong until proven right.

Application and Challenge:

Here are some ways to double-check our work:

Double-check Options:
1. AB vs. BC
2. Use a different person
3. Close your work
4. Use a different technology
5. Do a duck check
6. Get some help

Let's tackle these one by one:

1. AB vs. BC: We recommend you use different approaches. If you approach the layout task referencing A and B, double-check it from B and C, or C and D to verify that you get the same results— e.g., lay out a secondary control point from one point on the traverse and check it from another point.

2. Use a different person: If you are the one who performed the layout, you can ask another person to check your work.

3. Close your work: If you have performed a survey activity that can be closed such as a traverse or level loop, as a rule, close it. This acts as a double check and a possible adjustment when necessary.

4. Use a different technology: If you used a total station to layout your work, you can check it with a chain.

5. Do a duck check: If something walks like a duck, quacks like a duck, and looks like a duck, it might be a duck. If you stand back and look at your layout, you can usually find pretty obvious problems. For instance, if you laid out a line of caissons and saw one set of stakes 3'-0" off, it may be wrong.

6. Get some help: If you are not 100% certain that the work is correct or there is something you do not understand, reach out to a team member or a team lead. It is better to ask for help than fail alone.

These are some basic but beneficial ways to double-check your work. There is no merit to a surveyor coming out to the project site and doing work that is not double-checked. Every bit of layout work you perform on your project site that has not been double-checked is a blinking red land mine waiting to explode. It can cost the project two, three, four, eight, or twelve times the original cost. In implementing this, please also have common sense. We do not have to double-check the location of a temporary job trailer six ways to Sunday. Let's just use the right double-checks when it really matters.

Another consideration is precision. We need to constantly do double-checks when it comes to precision, not just large layout mistakes. Here are some examples:

1. When you're checking your primary control or your ties to the basis of bearings, shoot the distances between your origin points to verify.

2. Consider turning a rough angle between points if you have more than one to ensure that you have the proper basis of bearings.

3. If you have two benchmarks as a basis, check the elevations between the two, perform a level loop using three-wire leveling estimating to the nearest thousandth, and close your work.

Here are some rules of thumb that will help you to visualize and implement these practices:

1. When you perform a traverse for primary control points on the project site, make sure that you close and adjust the traverse so that each point is completely precise.

2. When you layout secondary points, layout those points from multiple sides of the primary network or traverse and accept the average of those positions. You will have a more precise control pattern.

3. Once you're set up on secondary control points, make sure that you are shooting distances from point-to-point and confirming angles between them to ensure you have precise work.

4. When you layout from your secondary control, you need to make sure that you start with an accurate backsight, turn your angles, and then check back into your backsight to ensure that the angles were turned correctly.

5. When you perform radial staking on-site, always check to a third point to make sure you have an accurate setup and angular reference.

6. Additionally, consider double centering, shooting direct and reverse, and doing repetition shots when additional precision is required.

As you can see, the challenge here is to always perform your double-checks to eliminate mistakes while increasing your precision. Anyone can be taught to lay out points. Only the best can do it with quality.

The Concept of Tolerances

Introduction:

Tolerances are a crucial subject in construction surveying and surveying in general. The entire industry is having a difficult time with this topic, and most surveying done on project sites is done without consideration of the proper tolerances. If we were to observe standard industry practice today, we would typically see a surveying team come out, set up on an unverified setup point, backsight on an unverified backsight point, and radial stake points with a six-foot prism pole using a single shot and using a nail or a hub with a general mark on it as the layout reference. There is absolutely no way a point like that will be constructed any closer than 0.04' in any direction, and will not be good enough for many applications in construction, especially primary, secondary, or working control. We have to understand tolerances for the work following us. We cannot assume that everything is general site work, and we cannot assume that everything is precision work that will be used for the construction of the building.

Story:

When I was a field engineer working with a surveyor on a large four hundred million dollar project in Southern California, we attempted to close traverses better than 1:100,000' of accuracy using a compass rule adjustment. We were having trouble closing to that order of accuracy so I decided to rent a total station. When going to the nearest survey rental store, I had a survey technician and salesperson lecture me on why I did not need anything better than a five-second gun for traverse work. I remember him telling me that I didn't know what I was doing and these types of instruments were not needed. I rented the one-second gun despite the surprising response I received. While using the one-second gun, we began closing traverses well over the 1:100,000' goal for accuracy. Clearly, a more precise gun performed more precise work. Years later, I'm still unsure why the vendor was so resistant to my use of the one-second gun. Why would they even make 1" or 2" guns if not for better precision and accuracy? Did he not understand what we were trying to do? I have tried various types of guns in dozens of experiments and have never found it possible to close a traverse with the proper precision and accuracy with less than a five-second gun. It's possible the vendor was used to laying out site work, general grading, curb and gutter, and things with very low tolerances. I learned a valuable lesson—we must be open to the necessity of tighter tolerances than what is typically used for site work.

Know the tolerances for the work you are performing.

Application and Challenge:

To apply this challenge, we need to understand what comes behind the surveying activity. If it is for something that helps the building go vertically, your tolerances are very small. You might be talking thousandths. If you're talking about work and control that lays out walls and columns, you're talking about a hundredth. If you're talking about laying out something that deals with secondary control, your maximum tolerance is 0.01'. If we're talking about primary control, your maximum tolerance is probably 0.02' or 0.03' within a traverse that's over 1:50,000' accuracy. Clearly, we wouldn't want to use general radial staking tolerances for precision construction work, and we also wouldn't want to spend the time setting a high accuracy hub and tack for staking intended to layout curb and gutter, general rough grading, the position of a trailer, or other general structures with very high tolerances. We have to understand the work before we go out and perform the work itself.

Suppose you see a surveyor radially laying out points with a six-foot prism pole and an Omni Prism taking single shots with no averages. In that case, you will know the inherent error in the instrument, the human error, the error in the rod leveling, and the error in setting the tack will all combine to make sure the point is no closer than 0.04'. If you wanted a point for secondary control that would lay out a precise building, you would want to see that surveyor verify the basis of bearings, perform a traverse, align the points and adjust the points to their proper location, shoot in secondary points with a total station and a mini prism from multiple angles, take the average, and then connect the points together with either a total station and mini prism or a chain while verifying distances and angles. This would ensure that you have a point within tolerances. We must be more aware of the practices that will result in certain tolerances, and we must know what tolerances are required for the work coming behind us. Also consider tolerance "gaps" between different trades and contracts. Sometimes the concrete trade has a 1" tolerance on an item per ACI while the facade tolerance is tighter than that.

We'll discuss more of the ways tolerance affects our processes and what this should drive us to do in the section "Envisioning Tolerances."

Considering your Surroundings

Introduction:

Your surroundings are a very key consideration in all that you do. One of the biggest complaints a general contractor will have with a surveyor is they do not consider their surroundings and will set out points that get damaged immediately. Interestingly enough, that's the same major complaint that surveyors will have with general contractors. The complaint is surveyors will perform their layout and expect the general contractor or the trade partner to protect their points. Then if the points get damaged, the surveyors become frustrated when they have to come back.

This is an interesting situation and the remedy is to consider our surroundings. If we are laying out points in a roadway where there is a considerable amount of traffic then we will want to have more sturdy points. We will likely not want to utilize hubs projecting from the ground or use lath in a high-traffic roadway. We will likely want a more permanent monument such as 60-D nails. Also used is a survey spike driven into the ground below the top grade with a lath that is pinned down so it can remain even with traffic or whose information is repeated on a staking exhibit. We have to consider our environment and merge field engineering with surveying. Even if the surveyor believes their work is temporary, their thought process should be setting monumentation that could survive for the duration of the project. That way, no matter how long or how short it's lifespan, the staking work will survive until it's ready for use.

Story:

Story one tells the tale of a surveyor who came out and set out the points in the only accessible way on the project site.

He laid out some curb and gutter with a 10-foot offset that landed it right in the middle of the roadway. Twenty minutes after they were complete, damage occurred. When I approached the surveyor, he said, "It's not a big deal. They'll pay us to come back out tomorrow." This is an improper attitude.

Story two is the remembrance of a project field walk where surveyors were observed laying out every single corner of a footing system because the general contractor had asked them to do so. This was wasting an incredible amount of time and money. The preferable approach would have been to set up working control points from which batter boards could string lines. The rest of the footings could have been laid out more quickly for the crews. In fact, in this situation, the crews were waiting on the layout the way it was being done, and it was taking a considerable amount of time to do it with a 4-foot prism pole and the total station. Even if this was done with a robotic total station, it would have been quicker with sticks and strings. We must consider our surroundings.

The site conditions are just as important as the layout itself.

Application and Challenge:

Ask questions like the following: Is this something that could be better done with sticks and strings? Is this something that needs to be done with a different type of point? Is this something that can be protected? Is this an offset that will work to protect the points? Always consider your surroundings and anticipate difficulty in protecting the points that you lay out. This will serve the general contracting team and the people using the layout and will better relationships between them.

Honesty, Integrity, and Pride in Your Work

Introduction:

One of the biggest problems that face us in construction surveying and surveying is the integrity and honesty used in laying out points and providing survey work. There is a widely known saying within field engineering circles (and should be spread within all circles) that honesty is the best policy. Honesty is when we tell the truth about everything all the time. Integrity is when we do the right thing even when nobody's watching us. Having pride in our work means we are leaving our signature or brand on a particular survey and control, layout or work. It is our personal accomplishment representing who we are and how we work. There will never be a situation where it's not best to tell the truth. Any hidden mistakes or purposely omitted information will eventually come back and haunt the project team and cost a lot more time and money in the rework.

Field engineers have been made aware of honesty and integrity from their earliest days in the business. They have learned even the tiny bits of dishonesty, lack of integrity, and lack of pride in doing work will come back to bite them personally. It's a different situation for a surveyor. A surveyor can come to do the work, take their notes, and leave the site without sharing information about a potential problem. But sooner or later, the project team will have to deal with it. That is why it's so important for a surveyor, who won't be on the project site at all times, to be honest, have integrity, and take pride in their work and what they are doing. We must have honesty, integrity, and pride as a golden standard in everything we do.

Story:

There was once a surveying team that came out and intentionally laid out a survey network at a 6-inch skew from one end of the project to another to cover a mistake where the initial control was 5 and 1/2 inches too far in the east-west direction from where it should have been. They falsified the coordinates and did not tell anybody. Later, when the project team attempted to localize a GPS network on those skewed points, the GPS network localized it nearly 2 and 3/4 inches in the wrong direction. This meant all of the curbs for hundreds of feet had to be ripped out and redone because it was laid out approximately 2 and 3/4 inches off. This was a mistake that was covered up, hidden, and had very, very costly consequences.

Your work is your brand. It should be done with integrity and pride in the end result.

Application and Challenge:

Honesty should always be our policy. Mistakes should never be hidden. Integrity should always be our course of action, and we should take pride in our work with the knowledge that anything we do is a reflection of us, how we work, who we are, and how we do things. It is our personal brand.

A Surveyor Reports Data, Not Opinion

Introduction:

A surveyor reports data, not opinion. It is important to look at the data in everything we do in surveying and in construction surveying. It doesn't matter whether or not we think we're right. In any case, what matters is the data. You can understand and communicate anything in surveying with data. Let me say that again because it's so important. You can understand and communicate anything in surveying with data. That means that we have to keep accurate notes and follow the right processes. Because we need to know every step we follow to arrive at the end result, we have to record data properly and have all of the pertinent steps listed. The result is proper information we can use to retrace anything and find the truth in construction surveying and surveying in general.

We must have data, not opinions. I can remember many times in my career going back to analyze why a mistake happened, what the current circumstance was, or why we were chasing a quarter, half, three-quarters, or even an inch throughout a project. Most of the time we did not have the proper data to track it down which necessitated recreating the survey work with a series of as-builts to find out what was going on. This could have been prevented if we had the proper data originally recorded when the survey work was done.

Story:

There was a time when we performed a traverse for a one hundred and twenty million dollar stick frame, multi-building complex for a retirement facility. We traversed throughout the project site and found one of the points was 8/10ths of a foot off. The surveyor came out and started asserting his opinion was correct so throughout the conversation I asked him to reference the data and look at the traverse so we could find out what was going wrong. He wouldn't even look at the data and collaborate with us. We, as a project team, were forced to verify and confirm that the point he laid out was, in fact, 8/10ths off, and we adjusted the coordinate for our primary control network. This wasted a considerable amount of time and could have been resolved immediately if the surveyor was open to looking at the data and tracing our steps instead of just asserting his personal opinion of his own work.

You can understand and communicate anything in surveying with data.

Application and Challenge:

The challenge in applying this is to keep clear and thorough field notes so we can always look back and be able to see exactly what happened, in our process or from a mathematical standpoint We can literally retrace when, where, why, and how things took place, and quickly find out what went wrong, or verify that nothing went wrong. This is a key step in construction and the solution is to always look at the data rather than opinions. Field books with notes may have faded out considerably with the use of tablets and data collectors, but it is still very important to employ methods to log and store all relevant project information.

Fixed Versus Growth Mindset

Introduction:

One of the principles we must discuss before going forward is the concept of a fixed versus growth mindset. This is very important for construction surveyors and surveyors in general. Throughout the industry, there is a tendency for surveyors and people who have been doing construction surveying and layout for a considerable amount of time to be fixed in their mindsets and therefore, come across to others as rigid or even arrogant. This makes for a destructive situation where we're not learning, growing, and listening to each other. The same can be true of construction superintendents in construction who are used to doing things their way.

To remedy this means everybody needs to adopt a growth mindset instead of a fixed mindset. If you check out Carol Dweck's book, *Mindset*, a landmark work on how to grow, learn and progress together in a team environment, it will assist you to be open to learning, to accept challenges as a part of that learning, and to be open to the opinions of others. We really need to focus on the win-win in a collaborative environment. A fixed mindset happens when somebody thinks they know how things are. They know what the right answer is, they are not open to collaboration, and they do not partner, team, or listen to others. If a surveyor goes into a situation with a fixed mindset, they will believe they are right. Since they don't believe they create mistakes, they rarely keep notes. They will not collaborate or combine their techniques with field engineering and the wisdom of the project team on-site. They will eventually be stuck in their own world, offend other people on the project and possibly miss out on work.

However, if they have a growth mindset, they will be open to feedback. They will be open to keeping notes so that others can review and QC their work. They will be open to retracing the data and finding out what went wrong or right, they will be open to the suggestions and requests of the project team and the field engineers on-site, and they will look for the win-win. We have to embrace this kind of mindset in order for us to be successful in construction.

Story:

I once knew a construction surveyor who would always fight with the project team. Interestingly enough, he did not have his surveying license and he had not been in the field very long. He was arrogant in his position because he felt he was "above" the craft, the foremen, and the project team. He had been promoted to the position of lead surveyor on the project site when all he really knew how to do was to operate the automatic level, the total station, and radially stake points at a good pace; he did not understand construction fundamentals. He did not care for the team well enough to collaborate on a good construction control network so they were always at odds.

I found this interesting considering he didn't have the experience to back up his attitude, but this is something that I've seen over and over on project sites. As soon as he mentally elevated himself above somebody else in a false, prideful way, he stopped collaborating and adopted a fixed mindset. This ought not to be. Anybody in surveying, no matter how experienced they are, has room to be open-minded and learn new techniques.

We must learn to have a growth mindset, even when we already know what we're doing.

Application and Challenge:

One of the best things that a construction surveyor can do is to merge their world with an understanding of general building techniques and field engineering. They should adopt any and all proper practices that will help them get the right points with the right tolerances on-site for the right people at the right time and protected the right way so they can control the "where" of their project site. They will do it as a team understanding that they ultimately win or fail as a team.

Developing as a Surveyor: The Technical and Professional Step-by-Step

by Brandon Montero

Being a Rodman/Technician

Introduction:

Being a rodman or survey technician is an opportunity to learn the most basic survey fundamentals including the thought process of the crew lead. The task load for this position often grows in complexity and responsibility over time but often begins with a simplified focus on the more physical components of the trade. This smaller scope creates space for the rodman to also pay attention to when, how, and why the activities happening around them, appreciate the sequence, and think about the logic in each step. It is a wonderful opportunity to become oriented with "how things work" in the surveying world.

Story:

This story is about Joe. The names have not been changed to protect the innocent, but it's such a familiar name I feel like I do not have to alter it. In the state of Washington, there was a new construction site with lots of brush clearing. No, not the little dried-out bushes that put stickers in your shoelaces; I mean 8-foot tall blackberries with thick thorny vines that eat away at your gloves, your jeans, and your willpower to keep going. For such an unpleasant job they would typically utilize a third position called the chainman. The chainman would cut pathways in the woods on a grid or radially from the total station enabling the crew to travel back and forth and perform a topographic survey without having the entire area cleared. The topographic survey would end up underlaying a civil design, then the crew would grub the area of trees and undergrowth. Soon, a neighborhood might be built, or something else new and pretty. That was Joe's position; the chainman. Joe would get to cutting the line with his machete, and every five minutes you'd hear somebody say, "Joe! That way!" Joe was engrossed in his work, but he was habitually headed in the wrong direction. Why? Because his head was down and he was losing sight of the team and the overall plan. Remember, having a simplified scope gives us two opportunities:

1. Use our thinking power to absorb the plan and process of the survey crew.

2. Take the easy route, switch our minds off, and get lost in the process of our work without learning.

Always absorb the environment around you and take the opportunity to learn what is happening and why it's happening.

Application and Challenge:

I would apply this challenge to any person at any position at any point in their career. At the moment, however, we're talking about rodmen or people at a survey technician level which some (including management) may view as a manual labor position—as if your only job was to take orders, load the truck, carry equipment, pound hubs, and write up lath. This logic could make someone think, "Well, I do all of the physical work, and someone else does the thinking portions" such as operating the data collector or going over the work order. My challenge is this: While you're in that position, take advantage of the ability and absorb the environment around you and wonder why these situations are happening. First, ask yourself, "Am I considering the big picture? Do I know what the big picture is, or am I just out here creating effort without understanding the ultimate goal?" Until the big picture is crystal clear, continue to ask questions. Get the answers you need because the success of your career depends on it.

Loading Materials and Preparing for Work

Introduction:

To truly prepare for work means you will need to know precisely what it is. Ask for your own copy of the work order. Studying it will often highlight the required materials for the day including how many of each is necessary. Don't be content to have everything dictated to you—take the initiative in thinking ahead! Try to anticipate what needs might arise and consider every scenario. Which equipment will be utilized? Are there sufficient batteries? Ensuring that the vehicle is clean, organized, and prepared goes a long way to ensure the smooth operation of the crew once they are on-site. At this pivotal step of preparing materials, the crew's success can be made or broken.

Story:

This isn't a specific story because I've seen it happen so many times. In my case, I've worked for companies that have done remote GPS work frequently for control networks for municipalities or the transportation district. The crew would get up to a site some *distance away and realize they didn't have fundamental components to fulfill their task such as the car battery to power the GPS base or the paint and vinyl for their aerial control panels. These items were unremembered because the task to be done hadn't been fully considered. A general checklist of preparedness might have been done, but that checklist wasn't related to the task.*

What do I mean? Here's an example. General task: GPS work should include a GPS unit and small batteries, hubs, nails, and lath. Check! But anticipating the specific task must go much further: GPS control survey will be four hours away setting twelve aerial targets. The base will be running a long time and likely at a significant distance away so the large battery is a better option than running back and forth to swap out. Let's look at the work order. Half the targets are on the roadway and half are in field areas. We'll need vinyl panel material for the fields, plenty of white paint for the road, and the panel stencil. Is there a chance we'll end up staying overnight? Should we bring the battery charging units? Do I have extra panel material just in case? Now that you know the task, it's a much different checklist, right?

Materials prep is probably the most insignificant part of our daily tasks from a cost standpoint. Being underprepared will surely cost time, efficiency, and money.

Preparing for the work means you know what the work is.

Application and Challenge:

For me, this is where it starts. Instead of viewing your role as a rodman in a labor-type (non thinking, non-leading) position, ask for a copy of the work order upfront. Having the work order sets you up to best understand the task. It helps create a state of general preparedness. You know you've got everything needed in relation to this task because you've seen the specifics of the task. Maybe the work order says things like "Set 18 of such and such" or "Stake curb along a particular area." Perfect! Visualize the things needed to staking curb and make sure you have those items in your vehicle.

Some individuals may feel like it's above their responsibility or overstepping their position to ask for a copy of the work order, but does that make sense? If everyone is expected to perform then shouldn't everyone on the team know the task? What could be better for the team? Asking for your own copy of the work order lets you know the task, follow along with what's happening and why, and creates the big picture in your mind to work towards throughout the day.

Personal Preparedness and Choosing Tools

Introduction:

Are you prepared to carry out the day's activities without multiple trips to the truck? Are you prepared for the "what If" scenarios common to your task? A versatile tool belt is best suited to meet your needs day to day, but a versatile tool belt takes constant thought. Do you have easy, quick access to the tools you use most? It's beneficial to have compartments or attachment areas where you can swap out daily or task-specific tools. Could you keep a stash of small peripherals like nails, targets, and reflective stickers in your vest pockets rather than need one and not have it? Think about constantly refining your tool belt over time and streamlining it to your activities. Are there tools that could serve multiple purposes or are easy enough to carry regularly to minimize unexpected trips to the truck?

Story:

I'm going to use myself as an example. First, I have been a surveyor since the late 90s, and the latest refinement to my tool belt was probably two and a half months ago. I noticed ninety percent of the time I was drawing my tape measure while kneeling versus standing during tight tolerance building control layout and QC. A shorter tape pouch allowed me to draw my tape faster without getting it hung up due to my kneeling position and it didn't slow me down to use while standing. Yep, it's that simple. My belt is always changing to suit me perfectly, and it's something that I'll never stop doing because I want to be efficient at the highest level. There's a video on YouTube called *The Lean Tool Belt* which can enlighten you about making those kinds of modifications. I don't like to carry more than I need because if my belt is overburdened, I likely won't put it on the second I get out of the truck. Since I want to be prepared at all times, I keep my tool belt and vest streamlined enough to be convenient to wear. But I do carry things that keep me prepared for many different scenarios. I also swap those things out when I know I'll only be working on specific tasks for the day.

In Omnia Paratus is the Latin phrase for prepared in all things. "It's in the truck" is one of the most frustrating things the crew lead can hear from the rodman. Always update your tool belt and tool organization for the day to be prepared at all times.

Application and Challenge:

Sometimes your truck is on the other side of the site and sometimes it's down the hill or parked off-site in a designated lot. Running back and forth to it would be a huge hit to production. Take personal responsibility for being fully prepared. If you personally know what the tasks are and what the big picture is, and if you know exactly how long or how many, you'll set your crew up for success. If the only effort you're putting into getting prepared is thinking, "Well, here are the things that I normally use," you're guaranteed to run into needs you didn't anticipate and cost the crew time and money. You're also creating rework on your most basic task—getting prepared for the day.

Envisioning Work Orders

Introduction:

A work order doesn't just tell you what and how many. As you examine the work order, can you envision the smoothest sequence for things that need to be done? Can you gauge your current place in the timeline of the overall project? Do you remember if this task was done before and perhaps need to consider billing it as rework? Can you envision what obstacles or conflicts might arise as a facet of this task? Are there potential questions or options which may present themselves you could discuss with clarity at the office before pulling away versus by phone from out in the field? Envisioning the process from start to finish will help you complete it smoothly when it's time to perform in the field.

Story:

When I was a party chief for a certain civil engineer, we had a folder in our area called the *Hall of Shame*. We would place the worst work orders we received in our *Hall of Shame* so we could take them out and laugh at them later. And by the worst, I mean that the work order was epically confusing or gave the least amount of information possible about the task, basically setting you up for failure right from the get-go. You would look at it and your mind would generate a big fat question mark as far as knowing what was happening and what you might need. Additionally, there was likely no map to tell you the location of the site. Most had no job name or number on them. I remember some of them being on napkins and one was on the back of an already used piece of paper with a big grease stain on it. You really had to wonder how little effort was made for these work orders.

I'm recounting this story because I want to emphasize that when envisioning a work order, you want to quickly understand what is required and then consider what else will be needed or what will need to happen to be successful? What will be the progression of the steps that lead to the completion of this task? Envisioning each step along the way and encompassing the entire workday until that task is completed is something that should be performed by the entire crew, particularly at the rodman level. What is *your* part going to be throughout the day? What kind of equipment might *you* need? As an example, let's say you are performing control work for a remodel which entails traversing through an existing/in-use portion of the building. What challenges and obstacles might you meet? What will each person be doing? If you can't mark the existing floors, might small adhesive targets be a better fit for control? If the floors are smooth, will you need a tripod brace to hold the legs in place? Will you need to mitigate foot traffic with cones or caution tape? This really involves contemplation and anticipation to envision how the task will be carried out step-by-step. You've created a method to be ready for those potential hang-ups and pitfalls, and because that prethought has gone into everything you're going to do, you're set up for success before you even begin.

Always ask, "What else could be needed?" Accomplish the task in your mind in the office before stepping foot on-site.

Application and Challenge:

The challenge is to constantly keep your thought process turned on as if it were your personal responsibility. Don't hand off the concept of responsibility to the party chief or crew lead. If you take responsibility or create accountability for yourself, you'll put everything you can into planning it out in your mind because you believe that it's up to *you* whether the task fails or succeeds. Again, the challenge is not to turn your mind off because someone else is taking charge. Personal accountability at this level requires you to have a clear vision. A clear vision requires that you personally and thoroughly understand the work order. It's all connected.

Learn to Read Plans

Introduction:

The plan set is often the only official set of information from which to build. It supersedes the work order, office calculations, CAD drawings, and any linework uploaded to your data collector. Looking through the plan set regularly, asking questions, and getting familiar with the way data is presented is crucial. The plan set is the source of pertinent data like your HZ and V datum, and it details how each discipline will come together to build the final product. Get used to comparing task items with discipline to ensure each contributor to the plan set uses the same information (arch vs. civil, arch vs. structure, etc.). Spend time comparing what you have on your data collector or in your field calculations to what is shown on the plan set. Do you have the most current version, the most current data? Learn to take note of dates and revision blocks, revision clouds, and RFI's. Use the plan set to determine your current role in the big picture, in the life of the project.

Story:

Oftentimes, we'll receive a CAD drawing and it will contain the same line work that was found in the plan set. I remember a particular time when they differed from each other, and I sent an RFI asking about it. Their response was that the plan set was the official version. However, after closely examining the plan set, I noticed there were differences between dimensions and line work shown for the same items between the architectural and structural sections. I went back to them and said, "Yes, understood. However, the plan set is disagreeing with itself." They took a while to respond but eventually came back with the final answer and it was exactly what had been contained in the CAD file.

I chose this story because, even though there are many sources of data and even though one source of data is intended to be gospel, we have to get comfortable reading the plans thoroughly. We need to be able to recognize differences from discipline to discipline, and we need to know which portions of the plan set have data that pertains to our work. This is an especially easy area to become shortsighted because we typically only receive civil CAD drawings. As a result, our mind may tell us there isn't more to be concerned with than the civil world and civil section of the plan set. Such thinking could quickly cause us to overlook items from the architectural, structural, or landscape sections that may immediately impact our work.

As you get familiar with reading through the plan set, understand that they are imperfect and you will need to be on a constant lookout for mistakes or generalizations disproven somewhere else. Look for opportunities to cross-check or QC math and dimensions you see throughout. No one else is performing this task. Treat this opportunity to better understand the project as your personal responsibility, and you will save the project from future mistakes, miscommunications, and rework down the road.

Don't trust anybody! Crosscheck and verify! Yes, we are contractually bound to the signed and sealed plan set. Yes, we either use or correct the plan set through that contractual avenue. Only by studying the plans thoroughly can we come to understand the quality of the information being published.

Application and Challenge:

My challenge, which has become part of my personal practice, is to QC everything you receive from others. In a scene depicted in *Indiana Jones and the Last Crusade*, Indiana talks to the person (Donovan) who commissions him to find his missing father and best friend. Donovan warns Indy, "It's gonna be dangerous; don't trust anybody." Ironically, Donovan ultimately betrays Indy and figuratively stabs him in the back. That scene plays in my head every time I receive a set of plans. I can't trust anything I'm looking at; nothing. There's a snake ready to bite me on each sheet. I have to know that I have QC'd it myself if it's going to make its way out to the field.

For example, I have grid lines for a building in the architectural plan set, and let's say I've received a CAD file of the grid lines as well. I will literally need to make a distance inquiry on every single line. Period. Making sure the CAD file matches the architectural plan set and the architectural plan set matches the structural plan set. Grid lines placed in CAD means I need to send an RFI saying, "Hey, I have these two grid line intersections; these coordinates in the civil drawing. Is this correct?" Or if they haven't been placed, I need to reach out and create the RFI and make sure that the civil engineer has actually coordinated with the architect to say, "This is where the building goes." Whether it's in CAD or in a plan set, I don't simply believe anything that's being handed to me. I need to have some way to QC or verify that data. If I don't have that, I don't trust it. If you do not get an RFI response back in time, you must get on the same page with the project team.

Learn the Math

Introduction:

Math is a fundamental pillar of surveying. Although surveying equipment and data collectors perform much of the math on their own, understanding why or how the math works allows you to envision each step in the process as you perform it. It enables you to plan the next step ahead of time. Remember, the data collector and our office calculations are not foolproof. If the data was entered wrong while in the office, would we be able to spot errors in the field if we couldn't envision the math? We must consider what the general results should look like in our head before the data collector spits out its results. Understanding the math gives us that additional layer of QC at any time because we know how to check our results ourselves and by hand.

Story:

I remember a case of property corners being set in the wrong place on a particular job and going back to the field book of the crew lead who laid them out. Unfortunately, this story is rife with missteps, but we'll just talk about the ones that apply. One of the processes was to turn doubled angles for each property corner to make sure that our initial turned angle was correct and set with precision.

I was in charge of QC-ing or trying to troubleshoot what had happened out there. One of the first things I noticed was I couldn't get the math to work out for these doubled angles. Hence, I called the party chief and it turned out he didn't know the math for doubling an angle or how it should look in the field notes; he just knew we required him to do it. He was simply writing down his first turned angle and then making up a second angle. Some of his calculated angles had been transposed in his head and turned poorly in the field. He even noted them incorrectly in his field book. Doubling his angle as a back-check in the field and comparing the result to his calculated angle on the data collector would have uncovered each issue. Not knowing or understanding the math and not performing the back-check correctly as a result left him open to creating lousy locations in the field and leaving them there.

Math is huge in surveying. It's literally woven into everything that we do. There are a lot of math-driven functions we carry out without thought like pressing offset on the Data Collector or drawing a line and snapping to perpendicular in CAD which automates the math for us. But if we understand the math behind each task, we will be able to catch errors as they happen. We will see them because we can look at the numbers and say, "This math doesn't add up; something is wrong. What is it?" If we don't know from the math something is wrong, the moment will never trigger, and tasks that were performed incorrectly will slip past us throughout the course of our career.

If we don't know the math, we can't check the math.

Application and Challenge:

Sometimes getting better at the activities you perform in your career means studying or practicing outside the workplace—especially when it comes to math. While you're in the field, take the lead in being the person who carries out the math functions and performs QC so you have repetition, repetition, and more repetition in learning survey-related math. For a person at the rodman level or even at the crew lead level, if you don't know the math for the particular task you're carrying out, and you depend on the Data Collector to do it or AutoCAD to work through the process for you, my challenge is to figure out what math is being performed and QC your own work at every possible step. A surveyor at any level should view this as part of our standard function—know the math and QC our work accordingly.

The work isn't done when you've finished performing the task; It's done when your QC checks out. I've seen so many crews run level loops or traverses and come back with math that doesn't add up. Essentially, their work was completed for nothing and would need to be redone when it could easily have been mathematically QC'd along the way and corrected in the field on the spot. But, you must know the math!

Learn to Use the Equipment

Introduction:

Once the above components begin to take shape in your mind, understanding the case use of the equipment is the next step. Which of the equipment is suitable for each task? What are the best practicing methods for using each piece of equipment? How do you use the equipment to QC your work? Taking the time to perfect the basics such as instrument setup and using the hard sights or updating settings such as temperature and prism constant as needed, can't be overstated. This is where your previous work of envisioning tasks and picturing the math in each step will catapult your ability to be a competent instrument operator. Don't be content to let what others tell you define your experience. Look for instructional videos, download, and read instrument manuals. There is always room to broaden your knowledge and grow.

Story:

If you are planning which tasks will be carried out on a project or if you're simply in charge of loading the truck, you will have to ask yourself which equipment should make its way out to the field. As a result, you'll have to understand the capabilities, methods, and overall logic behind using different pieces of equipment.

There is a "best tool" for each task, and there's a way to QC each piece of equipment. If you're not already on the learning curve and trying to understand how your equipment will help or hinder each scenario, it will be difficult to optimize your efforts and end product. I mentioned taking time to perfect basics like instrument setup, using the hard sights, or utilizing equipment. That's half the equation. Next, you'll want to learn the fastest way to use those basics correctly. How can you speed up your current process while maintaining quality? Remember, your mind should always be in the "on" position as you pay attention to your work and surrounding environment. When it is, you will ask yourself questions like, "Is this step in my setup really necessary," or "Am I creating rework?" Never be content to sit and watch, instead, think about the process, breaking it down and questioning the necessity of each step in your head. Is there a better way? Thinking things through forces new ideas and constant growth.

Learning the equipment is a crucial step in perfecting your practices and boosting your professional development.

Application and Challenge:

What does continuous improvement look like and how do you measure it? If you're a rodman who sometimes sets up the instrument or is in the process of learning how to set up the equipment, time yourself, beat your time, and then beat it again in a few more weeks. As you're operating the equipment, think about how long each step took or what had to be redone. How can you ensure you won't have to redo steps over and over in the future? Challenge yourself, set metrics, know how long each activity should take, and push to beat your own time every day. There's no true concept of growth without a way to track your progress.

Learn Note Keeping

Introduction:

Our field notes are often the only record of what we truly accomplished. Though the data collector logs store point values, our notes can contain infinitely more detail such as fuller descriptions, instrument and rod height revisions, and even sketches to help us understand how the work was carried out. Our notes may ultimately act as the exhibit shared with our project team or trade partners. Writing clear notes and well-defined stated values are just as important as following the correct formatting so anyone reviewing our work can understand what they are seeing. It's worth the time to take thorough notes and create informative sketches. A comprehensive sketch can even assist the crew in discussing the plan for the day.

Story:

I teach Surveying at Arizona State University as part of a Construction Management degree, and I have seen field notes from beginner level through expert level. I would say that many of the failures that arise in completing a task originate from not knowing how to keep notes. Sometimes the crew doesn't write down enough information to know where or how to start. The formatting for most note-taking activities actually prompts you regarding what information is needed next. When crews don't take the time to format their notes correctly, it is difficult for them to perform math, as it is unclear which values they are even comparing.

The way we store our information out in the field is everything so note-taking should be really one of the most fundamental concepts for a surveyor. There are many different tasks we do whether it's three-wire levels, turning multiple angles for traverse work, or monitoring over the course of time. For each activity there is a specific note-keeping style that will make sense, be the easiest to read, and be understood by others. When we can, it's helpful to study and utilize pre-existing note-taking formats. Since the industry is already using these methods, they are more easily recognized and understood. If we're doing a new and unique task, we'll be arranging things in a way that makes our data clear and easy to interpret, which helps the reader visualize our work.

I would add that when your work requires a deliverable visual aid, a great set of notes *is* often your exhibit and could potentially remove hours of CAD work on the back end for someone else to assemble a great-looking exhibit. If you have clear descriptions, clear values, and any pertinent math relayed in your field notes along with a great field sketch, there isn't much else needed. After an intelligent QC, these notes could be presented directly to the project team.

Always keep good notes. A great set of notes is your exhibit.

Application and Challenge:

Take the initiative to be the one taking notes if you are uncomfortable with the note-keeping styles of others. I subscribe to the concept that if something is scary to you, it's likely a necessary growth area. Any time there is an area where you don't feel especially capable, chase that area down until it belongs to you. There are plenty of online tutorials. You can look up almost any note-keeping style just by typing in the specific set of notes you're taking in a Google search and quickly locate formatting, math, and comprehensive examples. Additionally, note-taking is applicable to laser use and laser scanning.

Learn Civil 3D or CAD

Introduction:

A well-rounded surveyor is one who can knowledgeably carry out the largest variety of tasks. CAD work goes hand-in-hand with our product out in the field. The base drawing setup, point calculations and staking exhibit are often performed in the CAD environment before the surveyor even leaves the office. When their work comes back from the field, most staking activities can be QC'd in CAD or as-builts, and topographic mapping will be drafted out and added to our overall base drawing. This makes the fieldwork just one-third of what's involved in completing any basic survey function. Why limit your knowledge and experience to that third? Even in cases where we won't be the final or primary drafting technician, understanding the needs of the drafting tech will often change the way we record data. We'll truly understand what is needed to turn our work into a final product—which is very different from simply checking the box of accomplishing the fieldwork.

Story:

Here's a worthwhile reflection. Before thinking about learning CAD at the drafting tech level, I would say that for a capable surveyor in the field, you have to understand what is possible in the CAD environment. When you turn in your work (like as-builts or topographic data), even though it may be the plan for a civil engineer to design a site on top of what you turn in, they will actually work with the topographic map created by the drafting technician. They will start with that CAD data and go from there. They probably won't see your points, and they're probably not going to review your field notes. Your true client is the drafting technician because they need to turn your work into a product. *Their* product is going to be used by the civil engineer; therefore, the civil engineer is the client of the drafting tech. I like to think through this lens because it means I need to do everything possible as a surveyor to make sure the drafting tech renders my work perfectly. I make it easy for them in the way that I code, label, connect lines, draw a sketch, or take photos. Everything is geared to enable the success of my client, the drafting technician.

My thoughts continually go to the question, "How will this be drawn in CAD?" This means I must have a thorough comprehension of CAD. Again, I recommend learning the platform for yourself. Starting from a conceptual standpoint, ask yourself, "Do I understand CAD well enough to know how this task will be drafted?" If you're as-building a wall and someone is going to build a surface from that data, do you know how it needs to be drawn so that the surface can be generated with no conflicting or incorrect data and the drafting tech doesn't have to do a bunch of rework? These are all things that *can* be understood by the surveyor, and I'll tell you right now, from talking to many people across all kinds of different disciplines who work with a drafted product, that communication is *not* making it from the field to the drafter. The surveyor goes out and does surveying and he's thinking about surveying. The drafting tech looks at it as data because they aren't out there on the ground with you and it's not surprising your two visions don't match. Why don't these lines connect? Why isn't there enough data for them to draw a picture of this structure or create a surface? It's because these two worlds don't directly communicate with each other.

Always be thinking like the present draftsperson. Take the initiative to learn CAD for yourself.

Application and Challenge:

A great way to progress is to get your hands dirty. Take your topographic work home and try to connect your recorded points to see if it makes sense to you. Can you recreate the site—not just from your mind, but with the data you've collected? Could you teach yourself to create a surface, and did you record enough data in the field for it to be an accurate one? If you performed as-builts or staking work, take your data home and create an exhibit from it. Sure, diving in might sound a little scary, but there are so many resources available online. Creating a surface from point data takes about five minutes, without touching it up, to make sure that it is perfect. There are many things that you can basically cut your teeth on that will, number one, set you down the path of understanding how to use CAD and, number two, know how to better communicate with the people who are actually receiving your work.

Learn Applied Resection

Introduction:

Many trades use resection to establish setup and layout locations; however, results are poor because neither the process nor the math is understood. Knowledge of the process should drive your methods, and the accuracy of the points you select will define your tolerance. The more points included in your resection, the better your results (or residuals) will highlight which included point is outside of tolerance. For example, 0.000' is a make-believe residual. It means a location for your instrument has been determined, but there is not enough data available to backcheck or refine the results. What a dangerous place to start! As surveyors who understand the value of checkpoints and working within our backsight distance, we can be an essential training platform. Our trade partners, as vendors, often don't have the experience to train but are presently the ones doing it.

Story:

I have a story of malpractice involving resection that represents a fairly typical scenario. I was out on a site where someone had snapped chalk lines down onto the ground. A trade partner was using his tape measure to eyeball where the corner of a column would be by measuring over from the grid lines and trying to estimate an intersection for the corner. Without marking anything on the ground, he set his rod at that point and took a shot, and did it in two positions. He had an 8.5-foot rod so it was well over his head. I was a reluctant party to the quality of work he was about to perform so I brought it up. His response was predictable. "It's good; my residuals say 0.000'." He was very confident in his performance. Let's get right into two-point resections with 0.000' results and why we need to view them as a red flag instead of a success.

When you see an "all zeroes" residual, it specifically means there's not enough data to disprove anything. The only available mathematical solution is to hold the two positions. Whatever the error in measurement between those two positions, the slope transfers right into the calculated coordinates for the instrument. For example, if you measured half an inch long to both resection points due to rod error, without other resection points to prove or disprove your measurements, that extra half an inch goes right into the coordinate calculations for your setup. The data collector doesn't tell you which is wrong. It doesn't highlight which might have been a bad observation. It accepts it and maintains everything is perfect. If that half an inch made its way into your setup location, do you think you can layout anything with better than half an inch accuracy?

How do we understand when something is good or bad? Learn applied resection! If you incorporate a minimum of three points, the first thing you'll see is that you will have a residual that's not zero. You will be able to see how big your error is. Places where errors can creep into resections, just like everything else, could be the height of a rod. When doing any type of control work, the shorter the rod, the better. That way, any inaccuracy in your bubble isn't turning into inaccuracy of measurement. In this story, the trade partner also wasn't really shooting any control. He was just eye-balling positions rather than using something with a predetermined coordinate. He had linework for this wall in CAD, or rather, for the design wall in CAD, not for an as-built wall which is what he was attempting to create out there in the field. Yep, tons of little errors were creeping into this work.

If three points are all that is needed to give you some sort of residual, four or five points would help you determine which observations fit best together and which fit poorly. If your residuals were a little high and you had five points, was there any single residual that stood out poorly while the majority were really good? You could remove the poor observation from your resection and see how that affected your remaining residuals, as long as there were still three or more being used. There are many different ways to perform tight work when performing a resection. Just like any other system of averages, the more information, the better, to prove or disprove exactly which point is your outlier.

All zeroes residuals are make-believe. They don't exist.

Application and Challenge:

Surveyors, field engineers, superintendents, and owners can really set up quickly and perform killer work with resections, so I'd like to introduce the concept of resections—first, what it is and then get right into the story.

Performing a resection means setting up your instrument at a random location. In other words, there's no point underneath it, no rebar, no nail. You're just setting up somewhere you believe is a good vantage point to perform your work and you can see a minimum of three other control points with known coordinates. You will turn angles and shoot distances to the three points, and based on the known coordinates, the data collector will triangulate or resect coordinates for the position of your setup. If you have calculated the height checked as an option and you're inputting instrument height and rod heights, the resection routine will even be able to figure out the height of the instrument center from which you're recording your observations.

In the superintendent and field engineer world, resections are often used in conjunction with going vertical inside buildings or being able to resect from the edge of a deck to as-built or check control. Along with turning 90 degrees and projecting vertically through the sleeves, resections can be used as a quick way to come off of projected grid lines, get set up, and lay out Blue Bangers on decks. That's inside the building, and most commonly, surveyors themselves perform work up to the building footprint. What are some of the most common applications for surveyors specifically?

Many of our trade partners are already using resections to set positions such as penetrations to determine where their utilities go. It's common to see electricians using resection techniques for the stub locations of electrical bollards and light poles. You will see the HVAC guy figuring out where his overhead alignments run or turn vertically. It's become a common practice. It is also commonly done incorrectly or with extremely poor accuracy.

In the civil layout world, surveyors commonly use resection on busy or complicated sites. Too often, the primary control is set around the perimeter of the site. Once buildings and structures start going up, it's harder to occupy points on the extremity and see clearly back to the central parts of the site. When performing a resection, it's convenient to set your total station somewhere out of the way of site traffic where you know you can see your work and you can see enough control (3 point minimum, of course), locate yourself, and then begin working.

Resections are getting a little extra focus in this book for a very specific reason. Surveyors, field engineers, or superintendents want to be able to collaborate with or manage trade partners using resection. To do so, we must ensure our trade partners are using proper technique, especially when they are laying out components of the building or penetrations with tight tolerances. Here's the challenge for the rest of us: If you are someone who understands the math and process behind intelligently applied resections, spread that training around. Right now, the primary way that our trade partners are receiving any training is from our vendors, right? Our vendors are not surveyors or mathematicians. They are salespersons. They want to get you going as fast as possible. They may not understand the math behind the task or the tolerances of your work which means we have to look for those opportunities to spread information around. The success of any project is the product of all of the trades including all the different companies present on a site. We certainly do not want to watch other people fail when we know better and can provide assistance. When we see those trade partners using their equipment to perform a resection, maybe even asking us—"Hey, what are the control values? Can I have two control points so that I can do a resection?"—we should be cued right away that this person could benefit from additional training and could stand to really find success if we gave it to him.

One last thought, and it's a good one! On tight or multi floor projects, steer away from primary control set on the ground around the perimeter only, as this control can likely only be used from the first floor. Instead, consider setting prisms around the exterior of the project or beyond on the tops of nearby walls and buildings.

Jason had an interesting example in Downtown Los Angeles, doing precision layout for Ambassador High School, utilizing a multi-angular resection. In his example, he didn't utilize distances in his resection; rather, he performed an angular resection and used that for the basis of most of the layout and control work. In doing so, he always checked in to a ground point he knew was precise and had good visibility. If his check-in was higher than he initially thought (he knew it to usually resolve to better than 0.01') or if it was higher than the tolerance of the task, he knew we had a problem. Both Jason and I had used this on multiple projects with a high level of success when we ensured that the targets were stable and would stay put over the long term. Resections are especially useful and common in the industry, so we must master this concept in both construction layout and civil survey.

Plan Your Daily Tasks

Introduction:

Developing a plan helps you put your tasks in a clear order, tells you what, how, and when to perform, and allows you to consider the potential variables and roadblocks that may occur. It gives everyone on the team a clear role to prevent doubled or missed processes. This applies to the entire day from arriving at work through leaving work. Without a plan, it's difficult to truly measure your success or prevent yourself from going off track. Remember, the work order isn't your complete list of daily tasks. Reviewing the work order and performing the work are just two of the items from your plan for the day. For many, daily tasks extend after leaving the job site to define personal goals, family time, date night, personal development, self-care, and much more.

Story:

We previously discussed the concept of showing up to work with your brain on "coast" mode. You might feel that the person operating the instrument is doing the thinking for the day, that a rodman is more of a manual labor task in which a hammer is swung, no thinking required. In surveying, there is no such position. The more you give, the greater the success of the team. If you're "all" isn't focused, then to some extent you're missing the task, missing the priority, or missing the mark. Compare it to a water hose turned on to run freely and soaks everything in all directions. But when you focus the water with a skinny little nozzle, all the force will go in one extremely defined direction. The stream of water can accomplish more because the energy and force aren't being wasted. In the same way, defining a plan focuses our thought, effort, and ability to succeed.

Planning our daily tasks should show up on paper able to be reviewed and shared. A digital notepad or planning app is fine too. We want to make sure that we know where we're going with our entire day. If we only think about one major task as representing our day, many things will quickly fall by the wayside. What about the time frame? How will fitting in the smaller tasks affect our day and tell us how to utilize our time? Maybe we have daily tasks, but one of them is time-sensitive. We have to be back at the office for a certain thing at noon or it could be something else entirely. Really, we have to understand how our entire day will be built and make each component a part of our plan.

For many, planning extends past work and goes home with us. It shows up in our waking thoughts. Are we anticipating a specific task taking place at a specific time? Do we check our emails prior to the start of our work day so we know what to expect and can plan accordingly? Do we know who we need to communicate with? At the end of the day when we head home, have we created time slots or created intentions for our use of time spent with family? Again, we can think about it or we can actually plan it, create time slots, and empower the completion of each item to ensure they get done.

Break your day down into the components that make up each task and each activity.

Application and Challenge:

Do you already have some sort of a personal organization system? There are so many different kinds. Some people use their calendar in Outlook and others use Microsoft To Do. You may even see weekly and daily plans built in Excel with linked references. As the weekly plan is filled, Excel populates day-to-day activites on a different tab.

Create a daily planning and tracking system for yourself. There are so many applications out there that can streamline the process for you. Doing so may enable you to clearly see where you have been missing the mark and allow you to better achieve what you have planned for yourself. The ability to streamline, tune up, or focus your day only exists when you know how you're using your time.

Learn Applied Leveling and Level Loops

Introduction:

Transferring an elevation from the project benchmark to the site and from the site benchmark around the project supports the building process and brings an additional layer of QC to the job site. Understanding leveling philosophy, leveling math, and instrument setup is an essential component to the backbone of any survey career. Like total station work, leveling has its own field note-taking styles and best practices to make its final product clear and concise.

Closure and adjustment of leveling work drive accuracy. It's essential to understand error distribution, how to clearly publish final elevations, and how to ensure that information is distributed to the team. In addition, your final adjusted values need to be clearly marked and distributed to anyone who will be using your data or coming off your benchmarks.

It's a two-step concept. First, applied leveling refers to how you use your level. When is it considered the correct instrument to use for the task? How quickly are you able to set that instrument up and perform work? To grasp applied leveling, just like with a resection, you really do have to understand the math behind what you're doing. If you can visualize the math, it should tell you when the QC process is necessary and even how you would perform a QC.

There are different types of leveling field notes. There's the single wire and also the three-wire which allows you to measure distance in your observations. There are lots of different ways we might use the level, but there is a very integral second step in our leveling discussion.

Learning level loops, closure, and adjustment of leveling work drive its accuracy. It's essential to understand error distribution, how to publish final elevations, and how to ensure that information is distributed to the team. In addition, your final adjusted values need to be clearly marked and distributed to anyone who will be using your data.

How do these two work together? From a QC standpoint, closing the level loop is the QC process for leveling. By going back to our original benchmark, we have the ability to see if we created an error as we performed our work. As far as leveling styles, I strongly recommend and personally use three-wire closed level loops. Using three-wire, its field notes, and the math associated with its field notes, you can even see observation to observation if and where you've created some sort of an error as each observation is triple-checked.

There are many different ways to incorporate QC into your work as you're performing it, and there are other techniques in leveling. One of them is "bucking in" which is when you set up your level at the height of an existing vertically set benchmark. Let's say you have a target on the wall that's four feet above the finished floor. If you buck in, you can use your setup to create more targets at the exact same height without performing math. If you know the elevation of your target, you can directly subtract your rod readings to get a true elevation at each observation point.

Many of the same basic survey principles apply to level work. If you have a particular distance to the backsight, you shouldn't make observations further than that distance from your setup as your foresight. Once you've set those foresight points, just like in any other level loop, you need to kick a leg (move your setup), set up again with your newly set target as your backsight, and then foresight the original—closing the loop and making sure no error has crept in. Mastering applied leveling means an understanding of math. Understand the QC process, and don't deviate from those things.

Story:

I once worked with a company that had what I call "rampant elevation" problems throughout their projects based on the fact they weren't using good surveying techniques or good leveling techniques. A couple of the concepts include using the right data, looping through two benchmarks, using three-wire leveling, estimating to the nearest thousands, closing level loops, and making sure data and great notes are recorded. Those are some of the fundamentals. Most of us can reflect back on projects where the original survey data or the benchmarks brought in were incorrect.

The miscalculation could be six inches or maybe even eight inches. We sometimes experience ridiculously large inconsistencies in elevation around the site. In my opinion, this typically stems from the incorrect use of trigonometric elevations or improper use of leveling techniques and not using the right instruments. For that reason, these best practices can't be highlighted enough. When there are surveyors on a jobsite who are not applying the basics, don't know the fundamentals, or know how to drive accuracy and precision, you will have a problem.

Applied leveling means applying leveling techniques in a way that accurate math and QC are ingrained in the process.

Application and Challenge:

I'm a big advocate of three-wire level loops. You may think that doing single-wire is much faster, but my challenge to you is this: Get faster at doing three-wire. Similarly to figuring out the flow and other tasks, apply math and note-taking so no one is waiting. There's an easy template that works for three-wire leveling which includes someone walking while you're writing and doing math. That way, when they're ready for an observation, you will be ready. No big pauses and no waiting around. It really shouldn't take you much longer than any other method, and it's so much better from a QC standpoint. Doubling the QC is built right into it which doubles the data. Feedback on distance and overall loop accuracy becomes available to you. It's really a remarkable way to do things. If you're in that *faster is always going to win* mindset, take something that really can't steer you wrong and get faster on that technique so that you are always set up for success.

Learn Layout Basics

Introduction:

Learning to use equipment is one thing, but knowing the best way to operate it when performing individual tasks is another. An in-depth understanding of best practice in areas like setting points along a baseline, turning perfect 90-degree angles, working within your backsight distance, or when and how to use the plumb bob or rod all come together to create proficiency in layout. The approach used in one type of layout may be completely different from another depending on how it will be utilized during construction. As such, a well-rounded knowledge base will always serve you best.

Story:

Let's go back to the concept of building layout. When you're using a conventional instrument, you can go through the steps of turning a really fine 90, marking it, flopping your instrument, turning the reverse of that 90, and marking it again to create an averaged observation representing a true 90. Just performing the process helps you understand what the instrument is capable of. You'll see the less-than-perfect capabilities of your instrument reflected physically on the ground that you marked. You can even visualize how to correct that error out of existence. That's not something we typically see when operating an instrument robotically while performing civil layout. Often when we use the robotic total station to double an angle for us, it's not until we occupy our new point and shoot back to our origin that we realize, "Hmph, that wasn't all that accurate, was it?"

We know there was an error, but we're no longer in a position to correct it. When you do things conventionally, you get to see what the equipment is capable of and make the correction right then and there. Having experience performing the basics or conventionally performing work will help you gain an understanding of what any total station can do when you should expect it to be accurate, and how to work around it when it's not. With robotic total stations, it's become common among surveyors to not spend much time considering the actual capabilities of the equipment. We just believe what we see on the data collector. We let the robot turn its angle, assume the accuracy is top-notch, and move on. Doubling an angle using a robot is reserved to average the location of points that have already been there's no real system of double-checks or working the inherent error out of our work as we are laying it out. Remember, *don't trust anybody!* When we're in that mindset, we don't just accept. We must QC.

Conventional layout principles are an excellent way to teach a surveyor the true capabilities of their equipment.

Application and Challenge:

Building layout (or rather, grid line layout) is the best possible place to practice survey basics using conventional equipment. It's simple but incredibly precise. You're turning angles and measuring specific distances. There's so much you're doing manually, even physically, versus just allowing the robotic instrument to tell you where things are and accepting what you see. Conventional work helps you visualize and think about inherent equipment errors and how to mitigate them when carrying out tight tolerance applications. Conventional work even forces you to consider additional factors such as the type of rod that would support your tight tolerance work. My challenge is for you to work your way through the basics using a conventional total station instead of going straight to operating things robotically without understanding the full potential of your piece of equipment from an accuracy standpoint.

Envisioning Tolerances

Introduction:

When planning equipment and approach, understanding the tolerance of the task is key. Task tolerance isn't the same as your individual tolerance. Task tolerance is the combined tolerance available for all parties involved in constructing any particular item. To understand your individual tolerance, it's best to consider the accuracy of the equipment and/or the people following you. If an excavator follows you, will it really dig a trench to better than 0.1'? If the total task available tolerance for a wall placement is .02'," and only people with less precise equipment will follow you in the construction process, can you really allow the entire ¼" inaccuracy in your layout? A best practice is to utilize no more than half of the available tolerance of any task. To do so, you need to understand or envision what that tolerance is.

Story:

Early in my career, I worked under a surveyor, and when we were doing tasks like curb layout, he required that we set the attack in every hub—not just corners, but even points along the line. It always felt like a waste of time, but he really wanted to create an earmark for himself of accuracy and wanted our work to *appear* accurate. Understood. But I remember being out in the field and watching people follow our layout using a curb machine to lay the curb. They would set a pin at one angle point and a pin at the other angle point and pull a string between them, ignoring our points along the line aside from grade breaks, and the curb machine would just start going.

I always questioned whether the level of effort we put into the work was worth it. We should always be asking ourselves questions like that. What is the true tolerance of the work we are doing, and what equipment will follow our work? Do we need to dedicate more time to do it accurately or less time because less accuracy is necessary? All of these things are relevant to how we spend time on a project site.

Use no more than half the available tolerance of any task.

Application and Challenge:

Consider how often you ask what the tolerance is for each task. Let's say you're learning and your party chief says, "For this curb layout, I'd like you to be better than 0.05'." Do you know if that's the true tolerance of this task? What is the logic that drives that tolerance? Do you need to be that precise for every point? Is there wiggle room in some areas? I would say, "Do you really know what the tolerance is for each task?" When you have the tolerance described to you from a superintendent or someone else on the project team, ask yourself, "How much of that tolerance are you going to use up in your surveying methods?" If your practices or your equipment tolerances by themselves eat up the entire task tolerance, then all of your work would have to be performed to a precision of 0.00', which is extremely unlikely.

Knowing the tolerance dictates what type of methods, practices, and equipment you use and is always a question you should ask as you plan how you'll attack each task. I'm not saying to use all or none of your tolerance—I'm saying to think it through and be intentional in everything you do.

Learn Applied Distance and Angle Measurement

Introduction:

To understand distance and angular measurements with a total station, you must fully understand your equipment's specifications. The specifications portion of your user's manual will tell you the true accuracy of each distance measurement. For total stations, the angular accuracy is likely part of the model number and is clearly stated. Your prism pole may have a 40, 20, or 8-minute bubble vial which will affect its potential accuracy even when perfectly calibrated. Knowing the quality necessary for each measurement is another aid in selecting the best approach for each task. When more accuracy is needed, this should prompt you to consider averaging as an approach over a singular observation.

Story:

Let's think back to the concept of someone performing a resection and the data collector saying that their two-point resection was resolved to 0.000'. Is that number a true reflection of mathematical accuracy or is it just a number on a screen? Let's say you can turn your measurement units to show four decimal places on your instrument. Wow, measurements to the ten-thousandths! But can your instrument measure accurately enough to provide you with repeatable four decimal place results or is it measuring less accurately and simply showing you four decimal places because of your settings? Even though we see numbers that appear accurate—whether we're turning an angle, shooting a distance or performing a resection—we must stop and think about the specifications of the equipment and how we would apply that to *this* measurement.

Let's consider a couple more examples starting with the circular bubble vial on most of our prism poles. When the bubble reads plumb, it doesn't mean perfectly plumb. The rod is plumb as accurately as the 40, 20, or 8-minute bubble vial can measure. Even when perfectly calibrated, the circular bubble vial was never engineered to perform any more accurately than its specifications state. A five-second total station is measured only to an accuracy of plus or minus five seconds in either direction when it's perfectly calibrated. So "perfectly calibrated" is still an imperfect measurement. Keeping that in mind will help us understand when best practices need to be used to do better if "better" is called for from a tolerance standpoint. It will also help us understand how we're eating up our tolerances with the inherent error in our equipment.

The inherent error in your instrument may be enough to use up most of your task tolerance.

Application and Challenge:

There's always more to the story so consider what that might be for each of your tasks. Read the specifications of your equipment in your user's manual and know what you're working with. Your GPS instrument might tell you that your horizontal position is within 0.01' and you're thinking, "What a great day I'm having; every shot is better than 0.01'!" But what are the specifications of the instrument? The display tells us we're within 0.01' of our point, but horizontal residuals are fluctuating between 0.03' and 0.04'. The instrument specifications tell us horizontal measurement accuracy is dependent on a slew of factors like satellite placement, satellite availability, and skyline obstructions. We always want to be realistic about what we're working with versus accepting what is displayed on our data collector or instrument display.

Learn Double-Checks

Introduction:

There are many ways to incorporate double-checks into your work, including measuring from contrasting directions, using different equipment, having another person reobserve, and averaging as defined in the last section. Site conditions and the distance of the measurement will play a role in selecting the best methodology. For distances under 25,' a tape measure is a great resource, and for less than 100', a properly tensioned steel tape may be a great method. But if the site isn't clear and flat, oftentimes, measuring from a different direction or averaging will be your best form of a double-check. Double-checks may also come in the form of data comparison such as verifying that data from the plan set is consistent with existing conditions or constant from one area of the plan set to another, as previously discussed.

Story:

At one of our boot camps (an intensive technical and professional multi-day training), we had a crew that was learning how to use a total station. It just so happened that this total station was experiencing some systematic error in which it would return a distance that looked correct, but the next check shot would return a bad distance that looked visibly incorrect. This would only happen when the prism was close to the instrument, and they were losing faith in determining which shot was the actual distance. The crew was restarting the instrument, turning the angle repeatedly, shooting it, but they were starting to get really frustrated with this piece of equipment. In their case, the distance was only about 22 feet away, and at any time, they could have simply turned an angle, sighted a line with their instrument and pulled the tape measure on flat ground, or pulled their steel tape. Not only would that have given them an idea of the distance to go from the instrument, but it would have acted as a double-check when taking a shot to verify what was displayed on the instrument's readout. What a simple and easy resource that could have cleared things up for them immediately.

Everything that you do should have a double-check, and I mean everything.

Application and Challenge:

Let's discuss applications. When you're doing your measure up in the morning, and you take a look at the instrument, and you look back down at the ground to make sure the tape is still over the point, and then you look back up at the instrument again, there's your double-check. Yes, we're talking about double checking things as simple as the placement of the tape when using it to measure. How would you know if something went wrong when you've taken a measurement with the instrument? What if the person holding the rod took their deep breath and moved right at that moment? Taking a check shot after making your mark would both be a form of double-check. What if you're constantly switching back and forth between prism constants? You could check to an existing point or compare the distance with a steel chain. Are you double-checking your current settings? Do you have your instrument set to shoot a distance in an averaging mode versus a single shot? If you were laying out multiple points or columns along a grid line, could you measure distances from one end of your base line and then verify or average them from the other? My application and challenge to you would be, when you're carrying out your processes throughout the day, ask yourself, "How have I double-checked this data?" Maybe you are using a layout exhibit that's been created for you from the office. Are you double-checking the elevations from the point file you uploaded with the elevations from the plan set so that you're positive that these values are good? Or are you just saying, "I've seen this data once, and it's good enough."

Ask yourself: "What's the double-check for what I'm doing right now? Where is it in my thought process or in my daily work plan?

Learn and Use Best Practices

Introduction:

A best practice is a process created by taking instrument capability into account, selecting the appropriate system of double-checks to eliminate potential error, and ordinating the steps to eliminate wasted time, motion, etc. Once a best practice has been determined for activities that require a special level of attention, make these best practices a standard part of your routine every time with no deviations. Many activities—such as grid line layout for a building—string together the best practice methods of several processes like sighting line, turning angles, or quality checking measured distances.

Story:

I have a really solid history of not making mistakes, and it's not because I'm just plain great at surveying or because I have a wider variety of experiences than anyone else. It's not because I have a photographic memory or am amazing at eye-balling things. It's because I follow best practices religiously, and I don't deviate. If I know that pieces of information need to be checked, I never say, "I'm so smart and so good at this with so much experience that I don't have to do that double-check anymore." I don't excuse myself from the basics just because I have experience (which has created an error-free book of work for many, many, many years). I don't press the easy button for myself and skip those double-checks and best practices once I have defined what those best practices are.

Take time to define best practices instead of wasting time reinventing the wheel every day.

Application and Challenge:

You should be putting together best practices for the processes you perform regularly. What I like about this section is that this is where everything comes together—you know your instrument's capability, you're aware of tolerances, and you have figured out a process to make things happen the way you want. Now, as your new best practice, you string all that understanding together. I love the concept of eliminating wasted time by removing wasted motion. Now, your process isn't just intelligently thought out, it's fast! That's what makes something a best practice. It can't be beaten, it's flawless, works every time, and it's repeatable. What we see a lot more often is people reinventing the wheel over and over. When you take a cross-section of a survey department, everyone does something in their own way and it's different every time. If there is a true *best* practice, why would anyone do something differently if one way has proven to be the best? Have you identified best practices whether you're doing something as an individual or on behalf of a department? Are you advertising, teaching, and mandating those practices within the department so everyone can achieve the same level of success, speed, and precision?

Learn the Data Collector

Introduction:

The data collector takes the basic layout to the next level. Using point data and line work, the data collector calculates positions giving you the ability to offset lines, stake radials, layout stationing, and pull inquiry data such as distances between points or ID the azimuth of a line. Because it also stores data, you have the ability to record topographic mapping, as-built observations, or record as-staked positions. When performing large amounts of point calculations for layout, a drafting platform like AutoCAD is typically the fastest way to create this data whether it's from the office ahead of the work or from the field if necessary. However, there is so much you can accomplish on the fly right from your data collector in the field. In fact, there isn't much you can't do from a point calculation standpoint. Getting proficient with the data collector adds to your technical ability as a surveyor and is your first step in becoming proficient in any drafting platform. Once you're up to speed on both platforms, you'll see that the primary reason for selecting CAD or the data collector will be convenience, not platform capabilities.

Story:

While doing a topographic survey, I was working on one side of the street while my partner worked on the other side. Over lunch, we reviewed some of the work we had done that morning. The person I was working with was training at the time, and he mentioned that he had a rod bust for five to ten minutes of work, and when he realized it, he re-shot the information. I thought to myself, "Okay, that probably represented five to ten extra minutes of his time doing that rework," which isn't huge, but I showed him where in his data collector he could go into his raw data, preview his rod heights, input a new height, and drag it down the rod height column to the spot where his mistake was fixed. Doing that would automatically update the trig elevations and coordinates. This action took only about thirty seconds which could be followed by a review of updates in the point list to verify.

I also trained this same person at a time when we were shooting a whole bunch of trees. The company had employed a landscape architect so some projects had a special focus for surveying trees to determine which would be saved in the course of construction. I explained to him that he could set the data collector observation type to "distance offset," which would allow him to aim at the rod beside the tree and apply an additive left, right, forward, or back to the center of the tree trunk. With a robotic instrument and data collector, it is a quick press of a button versus writing a long description describing your offset from the tree and having someone correct each location in CAD, which is what he was doing. Because he wasn't familiar with the data collector, he was doing things much, much slower. There were special functions and advanced math the data collector could do, but instead, he was overworking the situation due to a lack of knowledge.

Another story features one of my most common mistakes. I brought my laptop out to a site, but not my laptop charger! Where was my "stop leaving the charger on the table at the office" best practice? The team needed some additional calcs on the fly and even though CAD wasn't available from my zero battery "thanks for nothing" laptop, I was able to calculate a pretty big cross-section of curbing just using my data collector. I had previously imported the site line work and the associated grade tags so I had everything I needed to know and I accomplished the work right there on the data collector! They are so similar to the CAD interface now that there's not much left you can't do. If you are someone who hasn't added CAD to their list of technical skills yet, getting to know the data collector is an excellent way to start learning.

Let the data collector handle the math, calcs, and edits so that we can focus on necessities like QC, process improvement, and our overall plan.

Application and Challenge:

Again, if you're a person who hasn't learned AutoCAD yet, learning the data collector is the first step in that direction because the platforms are so similar. Next, take time to browse the menus on the data collector. When in the beginner phase, it's really easy to just do the keystrokes our party chief tells us or to keep using only keystrokes we're familiar with. Browse through menus, see what other options and tools are available, and let that create the questions you can ask to grow your knowledge and ability in the future.

Learn Applied Traversing

Introduction:

In many ways, the surveying industry has sacrificed accuracy for speed and convenience. Although GPS has become more accurate, it is nowhere near the accuracy needed for precision layout tasks (such as grid lines) and definitely not at the repeatable level. For that kind of precision, traversing through your site control, recording multiple angles and distances around your figure, and then adjusting has been and remains the most accurate method. Using spreadsheets to perform your math functions and averaging and conceptualizing the order in which you turn your doubled angles converts this system of double-checks into a true best practice.

Story:

I received control data on a particular project from a third party who had gone out to the site and performed the control work on our behalf. Among other issues, the control points didn't agree with each other horizontally. We found discrepancies floating around e.g., a tenth here and there to eight-tenths. It just was terrible. If you were to simply accept that data or backsight one point, you'd never really understand the relationship of those things to each other. So to rectify or remedy that information, we occupied the stated basis of bearing, ran a traverse, adjusted it using double-checked angles and distances, and then sent the adjusted coordinates back to the third party for review. Their response was, "Yes, we accept this." Well, of course they did. All of our data backed up each number versus their GPS coordinates, which couldn't be proven.

Why would we want to start with or utilize unproven coordinates? Why rely on single observations point-to-point and in one direction instead of understanding the proper relation of all of those points to each other? In the story above, which two points should I have used as a baseline for my layout? Tentatively, there's the potential for the building to be off in location up to eight-tenths, depending on which we picked. Understanding the true relation of all of those points to each other and how the data could be adjusted was 100% necessary.

The accuracy of your control is the highest degree of accuracy that you can achieve for anything measured or laid out from it moving forward.

Application and Challenge:

If you haven't traversed your work and you shoot your backsight and get a discrepancy of 0.018', are you just going to accept that? If so, that means everything you lay out from there is all 0.02' off. What's your tolerance for this work? What if it's an eighth of an inch? Can you even calibrate work to better than an eighth of an inch from this control? You might be able to repeatedly from one point, but can you tie to that work from any other point on the project? Yes, traversing does take time, but without traversing our control, we're limiting our setup locations, allowing for possible errors to go undiscovered, and putting off work that will need to be done anyway down the road when accuracy is called. Traversing is the only way to bring it all together from the start and maintain a high level of confidence in your layout work.

If we don't yet see the importance, think of our multi-building sites. That bridge, that walkway, the MEP, the support MEPs— all those tight tolerance items shot from multiple locations will never fit together without significant adjustment or reengineering. A bit of advice for all you general contractors and superintendents—traverse work is rarely a standard scope item today in the GPS age. You will have to ensure that it is specified, or rather added to their scope and required by contract. Sure, there may be some cost involved, but as you can see, tying control around the site together is crucial. Therefore, we need to ensure the traverse and adjustments are performed.

Side note, there are apps and spreadsheets available to assist you in performing traverse adjustment. I was a big fan of Starnet years ago and often used the program to make least-squares adjustments and I liked the way it cataloged all my information and highlighted potential issues. More recently, AutoCAD Civil 3D has a COGO based traverse routine that allows you to input and manipulate traverse data. As simple as it has become, there's no reason to shy away from learning how to perform these functions ourselves.

Learn As-Builts

Introduction:

Things are rarely placed or constructed exactly where you staked them. Record data and tie-in points may not match the existing conditions in the field. Being able to relay as-built data from the field with precision is a multi-step process. First, the method of recording needs to support the accuracy of the task. For instance, if the task tolerance accuracy was better than 0.01', your process for recording the as-built needs to include a methodology that supports precision measurements. Second, the information must be recorded in a way that supports the creation of an exhibit that clearly relays the data. Is the description sufficient, does it relay direction, and does the order of collection support connectivity of the lines? Would a field sketch assist in making the work clear?

Story:

Instead of a story on this one, I just want to go right back to our previous discussion on traversing. You can already see how that would spill over into everything else you do. Here we are talking about as-builts but also readdressing tolerance and control concepts. Is your control better than the tolerance needed for the as-built task? Is the tolerance of construction for a wall you need to lay out tighter than the accuracy of the control you began with? It should be extremely clear all these factors work together, build on one another, and support that overall concept of considering your best practices and focusing on the need to use them in everything we do. If we don't, our precision and repeatability will be questionable. This thread will weave through everything you do as a surveyor.

I recall a project where a third-party surveyor was contracted to perform the as-builts for a crucial scope of a work item. When it came time to submit the as-builts, it was clear the data had not been recorded properly and another portion of those as-builts was not recorded at all. The third-party surveyor didn't fully understand the tolerance or the scope and it really impacted the timely completion of the project.

It is an absolute nightmare to be part of a renovation and realize there is no true understanding regarding where utilities were installed because the so-called as-built data is completely inaccurate. To seamlessly connect new utilities to those there previously, we must have exceptional as-builts. Imagine what the industry would be like if we recorded perfectly accurate as-builts to the same level of effort with which they were installed and everything was properly annotated on the as-built set of drawings. It would prevent so much rework and wasted costs for owners in utility verification work and schedule delays. I'm outlining for you and your crews a point of critical failure in our industry. I hope that anyone reading this segment takes it to heart.

Intelligently collected as-builts are crucial to project progress, closeout, and any future construction.

Application and Challenge:

I work for a company that has created an amazing permitting system. If at any time the soil is to be disturbed, nearby utility as-builts are reviewed on an up-to-date and comprehensive map for potential strike hazards. As a result, I receive as-builts of varying quality levels from vendors and field engineers, some of whom are relatively new to the as-built process. From time to time, the information they relay isn't descriptive enough for us to draw any kind of a picture. There's a shot here and a shot there. I could look at the data and assume that between those two points is where the pipe is and its elevation, but what happens after that? Where is the end of the pipe and where are the bends? Are there any dips? Always consider how additional descriptive data would paint a picture of what's happening overall— not just a snapshot of the spot where you took each observation. Perhaps you took a shot there because that's the point at which the pipe became buried. Is that information useful to someone else?

Okay, here's the challenge! Approach your as-builts as if you were using words to define each component of a physical sketch because, in reality, you are! The pipe starts. What does it look like? What is it made out of? Describe it. It's 8 inches in diameter, and ductile iron. After 10 feet, the line bends left, then bends again and rises a foot vertically, then bends again to take off horizontally to the northeast. Finally, the pipe terminates where it re-enters the existing network. Do you have either a shot or a description that backs up everything you're noticing visually? Where the line changed vertically, was there a shot or description of where the bend was and where it ended? What happens after it ends? What general directions does it travel from there if it's a T-intersection? Have you been shooting the top or the calculated invert? Remember, whatever you don't describe will be assumed, and that leaves room for inaccuracies. Ask yourself, "Could someone draw what I have recorded based on my data alone with no assumptions?"

Supplemental and Topographic Mapping in the Field

Introduction:

We've all seen a child's dot-to-dot. The finished product is angular with rough corners everywhere. The image is clear enough to tell what it is, but it's not realism by any stretch. Topographic mapping is the art of recreating reality, but points need to be recorded in a certain way and with enough detail to accurately represent that reality. This doesn't mean tons of extra time; it means extra knowledge of the process. This is my second plug for the importance of any surveyor to get familiar with CAD.

For instance, take something as simple as representing a curve in the field. Are you giving the drafting technician enough data to utilize CAD to draw a curve? Will the 3 points you collected make the curve appear tangent? Will it appear smooth or is more data needed from the field to represent the fact that the curve compounds? What is the best way to shoot a wall so the break lines and contours in CAD represent reality? Does the 1/4 crown of the road need to be shot? Will shooting the striping be sufficient to convey a grade? Can you see the way a grading network would come together with your eyeballs in the field? The more a surveyor understands how their data is used in CAD and visualizes the drafting process, the better they will understand what is truly needed in the field. Have surveyors draft their own work. Have CAD technicians and surveyors speak directly, cut out middlemen, normalize feedback for improvement, and create training opportunities. This is another huge area of disconnect and even point of contention for many companies, but the path forward couldn't be simpler.

Story:

Notice how all these topics are tied together? In the as-built conversation, we were thinking on a small scale about how what we recorded could be depicted exactly, with no assumptions.

I used to work at a company where I became good friends with their lead drafting technician. One of the things afforded me was direct, honest, and sometimes brutal feedback about the quality of all work coming in (including mine) so I could do better. I remember conveying that feedback to other party chiefs at the company, and they would respond, "Well, that's not what's on the work order." Okay, but what are we doing? What's the big picture? We're out there doing a topographic survey so that a drafting technician can turn it into a 3D model, and that model will be given to the civil engineer. Then the civil engineer will brainstorm his design, and the drafting technician will weave it onto our topographic survey so the design connects back to the existing world in all the right places. So even though our work order came from the civil engineer, we need to create enough data so the drafting technician can make a product that the civil engineer will ultimately use. It's kind of like the tolerance conversation. Remember the question, "Which piece of equipment is coming behind me?" Well, the drafting technician is coming behind me so the level of effort for my work should be, at the very least, suitable for their interpretation and use.

Please absorb the following: This way of thinking is a turning point in professional development that really differentiates effective surveyors from mediocre surveyors. Yep, totally just saying that out loud. What that means to me is this: Are you communicating with the right people? Do you know for certain the data you're recording is sufficient? Or does it go to the draftsperson (with no back and forth feedback) who thinks your work is trash and spends hours smoothing it out to look like their assumption of reality? All of this stems from how you visualize things in the field. If you're not asking yourself the question, "How will this be drawn?" you're doing it wrong.

Want to turn in the perfect product? Ask your drafting tech to be your new best friend, your mentor, and your harshest critic.

Application and Challenge:

If you can't visualize how it can be drawn just yet, get as much feedback as possible. Even better than that, draft on your own work. If you're not the person who's responsible for it, find out if you can be. Even if the finished product will be created by a drafting technician, why not take your own work home, connect your own dots, draw your own lines, and recreate what you did out there in the field? Doing the drafting end yourself will tell you quickly whether the work you're doing in the field is sufficient and highlight all the places you're wasting time or creating re-work for someone in the office.

Again the two challenge areas are:

1) Talk to the person who's actually drafting your work.

2) As you're learning or perfecting CAD, practice drafting on your own work. This will continue to highlight the areas you can improve and teach you how to make the process run quickly and smoothly in the field.

Learn How to Flow

Introduction:

On a two-man crew, no one is waiting on anyone else. The survey assistant has their own tasks, their own thought process and system of QC's, their own pre-work. They have a copy of the staking exhibit and access to the plans. When the crew lead is checking in with the project team, the assistant is preparing equipment. While the instrument person is performing calcs, the assistant is QCing the cut/fill they just wrote on the last lath and walking out to the next point to start pre-filling standard data on the next lath. The assistant is ready with the nail and hammer, taking a knee as soon as the instrument person is within a couple tenths of finding the point. Both crew members are considering the next move and the next point so there is no backtracking and nothing is missed. They are constantly QCing settings like rod height and prism constant, comparing grades from the data collector to the plan set, and reviewing work before they move on. Flow means clean/clear work, constant activity, and no wasted motion or time. Every item is considered and QC'd by both parties. New activities or unexpected tasks may throw a temporary wrench in the smooth flow of activities as you get coordinated, but once a crew gets started, if you don't feel like the perfect storm just hit the site, you're doing something wrong.

Story:

A long time ago I worked with someone who would hang out right next to me while I was doing calcs on the data collector. I would print out two copies of the staking exhibit, but he would fold it up and put it in his vest. He was a person who was just there existing on the site. He wasn't thinking about what the work was, wasn't trying to understand it, and wasn't brainstorming about what was next or how to get anything done more quickly. He was just there awaiting a task so he could do it and go back to waiting. When I would move, he would follow me around. I'd mark a point, and he'd put a nail there. I'd tell him what to write, and he'd write it on the lath. Sure, it may sound like a smooth-running crew when I say he followed me around and did whatever I told him. And yes, we got work done, lots of it. But what if he was in constant task-related activity at the same level as me? Thinking about where the next point could go, pre-writing portions of the lath, ready with the nail, plans out QCing cross-checking elevations, distances or my calculations. Our productivity would have been through the roof because we were both constantly working. No one was waiting or standing around, and there was no one with their thought process in the "off" position.

This concept of flow makes all the difference between those crews that really get in and get out when they're performing work versus stretching a task out into the whole day. Many teams really haven't hit that rhythm in the way they work together. We previously described the perfect storm, right? What is *your* role in that perfect storm? What could you be doing while someone else is working? Standing around waiting is never the answer. Whenever I was doing calcs on the data collector, the person in my story would sit down on the lath bucket. How do you think that looked to the other trade persons observing us versus a team with two people moving quickly from point to point, always busy and efficient. Our team was not amazing. Sadly, at the time, I wasn't direct enough as a party chief to suggest in a motivating way for him to think about how his behavior might be viewed by the project team. Technically, I was training him, but I wasn't training him on professional concepts that would affect the work flow or the perception of our professionalism on-site. I knew he didn't care. But you don't always have to teach someone to care. Sometimes getting them started on regularly doing the process is all that's needed, and soon your process will be the way they operate. The next time they see someone operating at half speed and feel like stopping for a teaching moment, they will realize how much they care now.

If you don't feel like the perfect storm just hit the site, you're doing something wrong.

Application and Challenge:

Ask yourself if each person on the crew has what they need to flow. What might that be? Does everyone have all of the necessary tools? Personally, I carry nails with me even when someone else is pounding nails. I carry a hammer and a tape measure so if they fall behind or if I've caught up with them, I'll go ahead and set the next nail, I will often grab a lath so I can start filling it out as they catch up. Someone is always moving. You could even ask the question directly to your team, "Does everyone have what they need to flow?" Maybe both people need a copy of the staking exhibit or maybe a plan set. How else could they look ahead or thoroughly QC your work?

If there are lots of starts and stops or a perceived imbalance in tasks, that means things aren't flowing. When it comes to scheduling systems in production and manufacturing plants, it's become well-known that the key to productivity is flow. Adequately prepare for future tasks, communicate the plan clearly, perform effectively, and get increasingly better with each repetition. The same applies throughout the construction industry. That is why our website and YouTube channel are called *Lean Survey*. All philosophies lead right to those concepts of flow.

Create Intelligent Exhibits

Introduction:

An exhibit displays facts about observations or data but also conveys important surrounding data on-site including how the area of work is affected. Information is conveyed in a clear way. Short, to-the-point descriptions are printed clearly, conveying datum, dates, and other pertinent information. Anyone on the construction site should be able to understand what is being conveyed as our exhibits often travel far beyond one recipient. What if our exhibit conveys a potential discrepancy? It will likely end up being discussed and reviewed by the whole project team, multiple trade partners, and sometimes even owners. Whether our exhibit is a sketch in the field book or a CAD deliverable, the same amount of care, attention, and effort it took to record the data should go into crafting the exhibit. Remember, if the information can't be clearly conveyed, it's worthless. We must view that communication as our direct responsibility because our job doesn't really end when the instrument case is shut.

Story:

Do you remember the *Hall of Shame* from our work order discussion in which we would receive low quality work orders, sometimes drawn on the back of a cocktail napkin or a scrap of paper with a circular coffee mug stain on it? How we'd look at the sketch and try our hardest to understand what we were being asked to do with no clear message being relayed? No one put adequate effort into clearly conveying information; instead, they were doing the least. In the same way, as we create exhibits, remember, no one is going to review the raw data from the field to better understand exactly what went on. Even a CSV point file as a deliverable is often not enough information to tell the whole story. We must think about the deliverable.

We may already be shooting enough points to thoroughly represent our work, but is the full purpose and usefulness of the data being conveyed clearly by an exhibit? The data needs to be communicated in a way that anyone on the project team can review the exhibit and understand exactly what is being presented. Their depth of knowledge and experience does not have to mirror your own, but no explanations should be necessary; they can simply look and understand. Every exhibit should be created the same way and be well-thought-out and clear, containing the appropriate amount of information so it isn't overwhelming and allowing the reviewer to visualize the work. Depending on what is needed, the exhibit could be a detailed sketch in the field book or a CAD deliverable. This is one reason a strong field sketch is so important. When a sketch is created intelligently, it's either relevant enough to aid you in creating an amazing exhibit or it is thorough enough to be the completed exhibit itself. We should pour as much effort into planning and completing our exhibit as we do the fieldwork, knowing that it's our true end product.

Your exhibit is the ultimate deliverable, not the field work.

Application and Challenge:

As you review your field notes and your exhibits, ask yourself if everyone on the project team will easily comprehend what you set forth. Can everyone understand what the exhibit conveys or will it take a surveyor to interpret the data? Let's say we've done an as-built for a steel beam running vertically through three floors showing how far it deviated from plumb. Those exhibits will likely get passed on to third parties, to the structural team, the architect, the civil engineer, their draftspersons, and anyone else affected. A larger circle of people than you know might see your exhibits so we want to make sure that we're asking, "Will everyone understand this, or just me?"

Focus on Aesthetics

Introduction:

As an owner choosing a builder, who do you think you would select? Someone who showed up in a half-tucked, coffee-stained shirt with a raggedy plan set and a stack of unstapled schedules and exhibits laying loosely in random order or the organized, orderly and clearly communicated plan and presentation of the next builder? Aesthetic presentation isn't knowledge, that's true. You hope the owner will choose the builder with the most knowledge or experience, right? But what else is being communicated to the owner through aesthetics? This person will communicate clearly in the future, this person is aware of how he interacts with others and how they view him, and he cares about those perceptions. He will care how the public perceives his jobsite. His jobsite will be clean and organized. This person is a professional, and he delivers a professional product. Is that how our product causes us to be viewed? Simple things matter such as the arrangement of leaders and consistently sized text, the removal of clutter and irrelevant layers and lines from our exhibits. We can also consider the arrangement of tools in our vehicle, the last time our vest was washed, and the care we put into our appearance—even when that appearance is working its hardest in the sweat and dirt of a fast-paced jobsite. Aesthetics matter.

Story:

I used to work with someone who was in the "new guy, chainman" position. Once a run of curb or utilities were staked out, it was his responsibility to stand at the end of each row of stakes, take his plumb bob out, hold it out in front of him, and make sure the lath hands had been set in a consistent way. If any stake wasn't perfectly in line with the rest, he would reset it at a uniform distance from the nail and plumb. The company we worked for wanted to create an aesthetic presentation that caused people to look at their work and believe in its high quality without question.

Aesthetics matter.

Application and Challenge:

No, aesthetics don't really tell someone that the work is correct, but it does communicate that the work was done thoughtfully through attention to detail and sincere effort. An aesthetic product looks like effort and quality. In addition, the time spent developing a deliverable that is aesthetically pleasing to the eye means it will be clear and easy to understand. You don't look at it and immediately think, this is cluttered, I'm confused, or I can't tell what's going on. You look at it, and visually, there's flow. Leader lines are parallel and pulled to one side, some are stacked vertically out of the way of important graphics, and there are no leaders crossing other lines so you can't tell which is a leader and which is a line.

Ask yourself if your product is as clear as it could be for the person who's going to view it. Ultimately, that's what aesthetics are.

Interpreting Work Orders

Introduction:

Work orders aren't always generated by another surveyor with knowledge of your methods or equipment capabilities. Sometimes trade partners will communicate needs to a project team that reaches out to the surveyor and important details fall by the wayside. Perhaps the task comes directly from the landscape architect or civil engineer. Never accept the items on the work order at face value. Ask yourself, do I fully understand the big picture, do I know how my data will be used, and do I understand task tolerance? Method of approach, level of effort and your end product can be wildly affected by these variables. Ask additional questions, explain your process so that your methods can be envisioned by others and they can weigh in if necessary. This type of regular communication ensures that each subsequent work order will be better tailored to describing tasks in a thorough and definitive way.

Story:

Let's revisit the concept of the person utilizing your work being your actual client, and continue holding that thought at the forefront of our minds while we're planning. How does that affect this topic? You, as a surveyor, may go out to "survey a site". That means a lot more than is really communicated by those few words, right? What's really happening? You're going to have a certain process to get prepped for the work, you'll develop a plan of attack, you have best practices in the field, you'll perform QC, and so on. In preparing a work order, if you described each of these components in detail, you could effectively communicate what needed to be done and also the materials and preparation necessary to get the job done. On the other side of that coin is the work order that does not provide enough information to understand the task or future deliverables. There must be enough information to allow us to envision our task and prepare accordingly. If we had that important information, would we bring in different materials to suit a tailored approach? Or would we record data in a different way that suited the task more directly? If we don't see the data we need, are there questions we can ask our client (the person receiving our product after it leaves our hands) to shed more light on what they might need or what would be the most helpful to their final product?

Never accept the items on a work order at face value.

Application and Challenge:

Do you know who's receiving this work? We get work orders from our survey manager half the time, or from a crew lead, but do we actually know who is receiving this work and do we know the details of how they'll process our work? I would challenge you to familiarize yourself with the people who are receiving your work, not just the person who is handing you your work order. There's so much more to be learned that would set you up for success if you ask additional questions and get the details. Those details and questions should be directed to the person who will be utilizing your work.

Communicating On-Site

Introduction:

Normalizing direct communication and feedback for improvement is one of the best ways to be effective and successful in work and in life. Some like to get in head down, do the task per their work order, and get out. Often, the fear is some aspect of the work will change and the day won't go exactly as planned—but remember, this is your client. Satisfying the needs of your client is your true task, regardless of what's written on the work order. When we get to the site, we want to speak to the project superintendent or designated task lead and the trade partner who has requested the work. Having them both present removes potential misunderstandings in the scope of work and level of effort. If something is different from the work order in scope or expectation of time, be ready to have a conversation about cost and priority. This doesn't mean you must know the dollar for dollar cost of each task, it means start asking questions. How can we bill this most effectively, how can we handle as many of their needs as possible within the allotted time or budget? When we're done, and before we pack up, we should have both of them review our work. Ask if everything necessary is there. Ask if it can be clearly understood. If you know paint or stakes will be hard to maintain due to foot or equipment traffic, a follow-up staking exhibit preserves your communication. Ask what can be done better, and get to know your trade partners and project teams so they feel your support. When we earn the trust of a client, we earn their business and their respect as professionals.

Story:

The scenario of communicating efficiently with our trade partners and project teams is not something that happens often on our job sites. Some surveyors don't want things to change from the stated work order because they have a plan or expectation on time and they don't want that expectation disrupted. Other surveyors don't feel they're empowered to talk about changes in scope and budget. The survey project manager may be so concerned with going over budget they may have communicated a blanket "No extras, no deviations" to their crews. As a result, they're afraid to have those conversations and stick with the "get in, get out" mentality. Instead, we want to instruct our crews around having intelligent conversations with the project team, about modifying scope while maintaining budget, or recouping budget when extras are necessary. Why is it so important that we're ready to be flexible every time we enter the site? Remember, we have a client that we are ultimately serving. We're not just checking the box of fulfilling a work order from a conceptual standpoint. We have to please this client with a job well done that adds value, is cost effective, and can be used to clearly and efficiently construct the product.

Open communication builds trust and respect.

Application and Challenge:

We talked about inefficient versus efficient communicating costs so now, let's get back to communicating our product effectively. The "get in, get out" crew leaves their site and immediately the superintendent is calling the office saying, "Hey, this isn't done!" or "Hey, I needed something else!" Maybe the trade partner who requested the work is calling you and saying, "I don't understand this." I can think of an instance where a survey crew laid out a curb, and the curb had little curb cuts where water was supposed to flow through the parking lot. They set stakes at the centerline of the cut that simply read "curb cut." The concrete crew interpreted the stake to represent the edge of the curb cut instead and assumed the rest. They constructed the pour-in-place curb with their assumed curb cut locations, but when the concrete valley gutters were staked, nothing lined up. It's easy to point a finger and say, "They shouldn't have assumed." It might even be easy to assign the modification or replacement costs to the concrete company. But wouldn't it have been even easier if you communicated what you staked on an exhibit and done a quick job walk with the person using your work? You would have had the "What does this stake mean?" conversation then and there or "What does this acronym mean on your stakes?" If they literally forgot everything you said, the staking exhibit would clear up anything and everything. No rip out and replace, no finger pointing down the road, no bad blood between trade partners.

In this way everyone is on the same page. Yes, those things take a few extra minutes from a time standpoint, but they ensure what you meant is interpreted by the people utilizing the work so in reality, it's a necessity not an extra. My challenge is to question whether we have these systems actively in place and are providing the training necessary to do them effectively. Meet with the project team beforehand, listen to needs, adjust if necessary, communicate your work effectively, and do a final review with a job walk.

Be Personally Organized

Introduction:

If just the phrase "getting organized" sounds difficult to you, it's likely because you've identified the feeling you will have to do things drastically different in the future to be organized and stay organized. Sure, getting started is often the hardest part because you need to find a system that works for you. Once a personal organization system is in place or is being practiced with repetition, it becomes easier and easier to maintain and will end up being less work. That sounds great, but how about we start small? Have a morning routine. Get out of bed, get prepared mentally, review the day, and center yourself. Maybe you can do this while you're enjoying your cup of coffee. Often this is more an exercise in having clear intentions than it is effort. Think about how you would like to organize your day. What do you want to accomplish, and what order makes the most sense according to your priorities? Write the plan down. This might be on paper or in an app on your phone - but a physical representation of your plan is essential. If you haven't created a plan, how can you track whether you successfully completed your intentions for the day and completed them in the order you intended? If you get off track, you have your plan available for reference to get you back on track quickly. Plan buffer time so that if your schedule gets momentarily derailed by an emergency, it's possible to recover. Take note of the things that throw you off schedule most often and better plan for them in your schedule. Along with optimizing your time, keep your vehicle and tools organized as well as your desk space and your computer desktop so you can work efficiently in an environment that's ready for you to be effective.

Story:

This story is about a pretty small topic, but I'd like you to think about the potentially big impact. During my first summer internship for a civil engineer in the Seattle area, we had work vans instead of trucks. Each of the vans had a little trash can to throw trash, hubs that broke, food, and anything else. I can recall my new crew rolling up to the jobsite, including a party chief who was not organized in any way, shape, or form conceivable in the universe. The truck was a mess with tools everywhere and no rhyme or reason as to where things were kept. As we parked, the superintendent came walking up to the van and the party chief got out to open the sliding door to get his plan set. When he slid it open, his trash can was situated by design right next to the door, and it tipped over, spilling out all the trash. As I scrambled to clean up, I remember the look on the superintendent's face as he took in the scene of trash everywhere and the disarray of tools in the back. He had to have been thinking, "Who are these knuckleheads that just got to my jobsite?" The superintendent identified the party chief as a person who was not used to working in an organized manner. He knew disorganization meant this particular party chief would probably take longer getting things arranged and carrying out tasks, maybe even miss potential issues or errors because he was used to working chaotically. The superintendent actually called our office with his feedback and to ask that this party chief didn't return. Ouch!

Do you have to move trash out of your way every time you want the hammer that goes on your toolbelt? Are your tools in an ill-conceived place that costs you extra time searching or getting prepared each day? So many of those little things matter and add up to how we spend time throughout our day. Going back to the concept of your day—how you "intend" for it to go—what are you doing physically from a task, task order, or equipment organization standpoint to make sure things flow? If you haven't dictated how things will go intentionally, your day will always be the result of whatever outlying circumstances are at work instead. I just got this email, I'm derailed. I just got this phone call, I'm derailed. They added an unexpected task, I'm derailed.

Think back to the concept of having buffer time intentionally planned so that as those little things come up—and they will—there is response time built in to get you back on track as soon as possible. The alternative is literally having an entire day plan ruined by a five-minute derailment to your task load.

Organize your day; make a schedule and stick to it.

Application and Challenge:

From a challenge standpoint, ask yourself if you really have a personal organization system, a physical plan, or is it all in your head? If you find you just accomplish things throughout the day that you have been told to do, and accomplish them whenever you're told to do them, ask yourself how much more effective you would be with a well-defined day plan made up of your own priorities. It's time to create a physical planning system that you refer to and say, "This is what's next, and this is how much time I've allotted to this particular task." If anything goes off track or overtime, you can immediately look at your day and figure out where and how you will get back on track. You can even plan time away from work while you are at home with family. Time spent working on hobbies, time playing with kids, anything you truly want to accomplish should be planned intentionally. Our personal organization is the direct measure of our effectiveness.

Plan Your Work

Introduction:

Planning your work is where best practice, clear communication, aesthetics, flow, and organization all come together. Each previously discussed concept needs to be part of the way you plan your work. It takes time and effort to create and deliver a truly comprehensive product. If we haven't planned time to be thorough, we won't be. If we haven't made it our goal to only utilize best practices, we'll choose the easiest way instead. If we haven't decided that our real work order is based on an in-person conversation, we won't take the time to have it or to ask additional questions. If we care more about budget than effectiveness, we'll never learn how to merge the two. All these steps are part of the planning process and play a fundamental role in becoming a true professional.

Story:

Let's say I'm going to train a field engineer on the principles of grid line layout. Nothing sets us up for success and flow like stopping to review exactly what the work will entail. This means going over each step in the overall process, likely drawing a field sketch of what we're about to do, using the data collector to show the field engineer the best routine to carry out the work efficiently, or even reviewing the note-taking style. When you stop and create a thorough plan, everything that needs to happen is fresh in your mind. You know what should happen, you know how it should look, you know the components, and the steps. As a result, it's so much easier for the plan to come together in the end versus regularly stopping to wonder, "What's my next step? Do I actually have what I need? Do I know the best way to do it?" Rather, the work is planned.

If you haven't planned time to be thorough, you won't be.

Application and Challenge:

Notice the first paragraph of this section stated, "Each previously discussed concept needs to be a part of the way you plan your work." Let's think about the previous concepts for a moment. Communication - What can you plan to ensure you communicate effectively? Is aesthetics part of your plan? How are you planning to make this a really great aesthetic product? What actions will you take to make sure that happens? Flow - Are you talking about concepts of flow with your teammates? Are you designating specific tasks that weave into the overall plan to make sure you flow as a team? These things don't just happen. They all need to be an independent part of the conversation as you put together your plan of work for the day.

Consider creating a system of checkboxes to help you plan best practice, communication, aesthetics, flow, and organization. Create a routine around the way the plan is to be shared. Vocalize the plan and ensure it's understood so you have buy-in from all involved. Finally, make sure each person understands and is prepared for their role. In this way the team will move forward as one to carry what has been meticulously planned.

Listening to the Site - Future Needs

Introduction:

In addition to one-on-one conversations about future needs, we should be the eyes and ears of the project team while on-site. Perhaps we could take note of what needs to be moved to support an upcoming task. Maybe we see areas where the site fill hasn't been cut close enough to grade for the single set of stakes defined in the scope. We may have a great plan to control grid lines from outside the building, but what about when it goes vertical? Observing items which might be difficult or confusing to stake in the plan set could start a conversation about how they will be calculated or what kind of exhibit should support the work. No matter our role, we want to have our eyes open and our minds turned on and active as we observe the site and brainstorm on future needs. Compare progress to the plan set. It's all there; the future is written if you know where to look. Our constant attention to future needs not only allow us to get a jump on preparing work, but can also spark conversations that help us prepare the site, make intelligent decisions about cost, and envision future obstacles so they can be removed before they have a chance to disturb progress.

Story:

I would suggest the metaphor of watching someone walking towards an open trench and thinking to yourself, "I see the trajectory of this person. Their eyes are clearly fixed somewhere other than this trench, so I know what's going to happen. I can either watch it happen or I can intervene and alert them about what the future may have in store." Alternatively, you could just not pay attention to the people around you or the site—and they'll just go on walking into trenches left and right with no feedback or foresight.

Imagine a project where there's been a lot of rain. Heavy equipment has rolled through an area and it's no longer rough graded and ready for staking, but you've been called out to stake that area specifically. As you go out to look at the site, you know in advance what's going to happen. You'll set all the stakes and the guy coming to pour the curb will say the ground's not ready and refuse to start forming. They'll end up rough grading it again so they're only going to use a few of the stakes that you set. That means they will call you out to re-stake in the future. Does the project team know any of this? Is that scenario what the project team would want? Do you know best what the trajectory and outcome is? Yes, you do. So when there's an obstacle in your trajectory, it's time to talk to the project team and say, "This area? It's not ready from a grading standpoint. Let me do some minimal rough staking, get it through grading, avoid a full re-stake and the potentially lost time." You've listened to the actual needs of the site, and now from a cost standpoint, deviation will be minimum. Maybe there are even some other things you can do on-site to make your visit worthwhile that are billable and within the scope. Yes, just having your eyes open and looking for ways to create feedback or communicate site needs can make you a valuable part of the project team. Ask yourself, "Is this task going to turn out the way they planned? If not, am I communicating those things back to the project team?"

It's our role to facilitate the project, no matter what our specific task is. It's always our role to be helpful.

Application and Challenge:

Make it your responsibility to create communication about future needs on the site. If you're somebody who is just getting started in this area, take some time as you're planning your work to think about and consider future needs. What kind of feedback are you getting from the site?

Do you see that this task is going to go well? Do you see potential obstacles you can communicate? In intentionally creating time to observe the project, you'll create a system where you regularly get feedback from your surroundings. If you're not looking, and you haven't made the time, then you simply won't get the feedback.

Does that Sound Right?
Does that Look Right?

Introduction:

The cut on the last stake was C-0.51 to Top Curb. This stake is C-0.02. Does that sound right? No? Okay, let's start our process of elimination. Is there really a 0.5' difference shown in the plan set grades? Would it create an issue if there was? Is there a feature here with a 0.5' grade break that I need to describe better on the lath? Does that look right? Is my rod height entered correctly? Did the existing ground change by 0.5' visually to support the change in my cut/fill? All of the above are questions we can ask ourselves when something doesn't look or sound quite right. When we calculate an offset and walk out to it, does it line up with other similar offsets? If not, was it supposed to? After you've staked a complicated feature, back up and look at your stakes from the viewpoint of a first-time observer. Do the stakes make sense? Would it guide you to the right conclusion if you were the trade partner using it as a guide? Once again, there is no position on the crew in which the brain can coast through the day. The QC process never ends, and staying alert and attentive to how things look and sound as we're working is a primary component of that mindset.

Story:

This scenario happened while I was working with someone just learning to lay out curbing. They were running the data collector and robotic equipment and I was pounding hubs and writing up the lath. I encountered a situation where the ground was nice and flat and then one offset stake along the curb was a fill of 0.80' to the top of the curb, and the next stake was a fill of 0.30'. I was anticipating a straight, flat curb running along the clean, flat ground so I thought, "What feature has changed half a foot if this ground is flat? Is there a slope here? What's going on?" He read me the description for that stake and I realized there was nothing in the description that supported a special feature having a half foot difference. The voice in my head thought, "What else could be causing this? Something looks wrong. Something sounds wrong." First, I started communicating my findings to the team so that two people could brainstorm the issue. Upon mentioning the half a foot, he realized he had changed his rod height and didn't update it in the data collector, ultimately creating a half a foot grade change difference that didn't really exist. Do you see what led to this resolution? The key started with me creating a mental picture of the work. Because I knew what the curb should have looked like when it was done, as soon as my mental picture no longer agreed with the numbers I was being read, the process of elimination began. Is this change in the cut/fill because of the existing ground? No. Does the description call for a feature that's half a foot lower? No. Are the published grades half a foot lower? No. Is the rod height off? Yes! I cannot overstate the concept of having your brain turned on and thinking, "What's happening right now? What will the feature I'm laying out look like? Does what I see support that? What math is happening right now? Is what I'm hearing in agreement?"

Comparing what we see and hear to our mental image of the work catches just about every imaginable error. But we need enough good data to create the image and we must have our thought process running at all times. When we encounter things like having the wrong prism constant or a backsight that checked on your last visit, but doesn't today means we should take notice and act. All the mistakes that can be made in the field are communicating themselves to you, but if you're not listening for that information and you're not asking the right questions, you will miss them and you will create mistakes.

The QC process never ends. Staying alert and attentive to how things look and sound as we're working is THE primary component of QC.

Application and Challenge:

Whoever you currently think is responsible for catching errors and mistakes, replace them in your head with yourself. No matter who you are, make it your job to catch errors in the field before the data collector and before the post processor in the office. You should be able to see them (observe the site), hear them (does the description fit the staking?) and think about them (does the math fit the scenario?). My challenge for you is to catch them before they're uncovered by someone else.

Do Your Mental Checklists

Introduction:

We've discussed planning your day, morning prep and envisioning tasks. Each one of these is essential and part of your system of back-checks. You read through the work order, compare what you have read to your mental checklist and ask, "Is everything I need spelled out here?" Once the vehicle is loaded for the day's tasks, run through that mental checklist. Is everything accounted for? What other needs could arise? As you work through each task, run through the flow checklist in your mind, run through your list of responsibilities and best practices, run through your deliverable. Is anything missing from your work, from your notes, from your sketch? It's a good practice to always know where you are in the overall scheme of things. Ask yourself, "Is this where I'm supposed to be? Am I missing anything?" Surveying is a profession of awareness. We must give our mind metrics to measure against to constantly ensure nothing is slipping past our attention. In this way, our checklists keep us on target.

Story:

Let's set up some groundwork for the challenge that follows. Where does a mental checklist come from? You'll need to understand the work you've been tasked with as well as what's needed by the person you're doing it for. You have to know what you're going to do and how you plan to do it. Your mental checklist is probably something that needs to appear physically on paper, at least once. What do I mean? Write it out, examine it, and make sure nothing is missing. Then it can be committed to memory as a mental checklist. Better yet, could you create physical checklists that could be shared with others to keep everyone on the same page? You know physically what you're going to do and then in the future, you can refer back to that list mentally. Ask yourself if you've considered the big picture. Do you know all the tasks that will be part of the big picture? And what would the mental checklist for each of those tasks be? Let's pick this up in the application and challenge section.

The consistent use of checklists helps us ensure that nothing slips past our attention.

Application and Challenge:

Your challenge is to write down the big picture and then break it up into tasks. Next break those tasks down into individual checklists. Create a physical reference you can see, remember, and share with others. You will absolutely flesh out and build on your checklists as time goes on, but creating a physical reference gives you a starting point, allows you to get feedback from others, and gives you something to visualize from memory.

Always Consider Cost

Introduction:

To consider cost, you must be aware of the budget. Unless you created the budget, you will likely have to ask to be made aware of expectations regarding cost, hours, or mobilizations. Who do you think I'm talking to when I make this statement? You, the crew lead! You, the technician! Perhaps there is an expectation of the amount of stakes your crew will set in an eight hour day, and an expectation of how many stakes it will take to accomplish each task. Let's say a quick little side task is added by the superintendent that will require half the amount of stakes you typically set in a day. Do you know your crew's hourly billing rate? If so, that's your billing rate times four as the approximate cost for this task. It's not such a quick little task anymore, is it? When additional tasks are added to your plate, find out before commencing how they will be budgeted. Will this be charged separate from your primary task? If so, how will it be tracked to differentiate your extra work from budgeted scope items? If it's to be bundled with your primary task, is there enough money in the budget to support that? Each of us should know these answers from the survey manager straight through to the technician. And if we don't, we have to take the initiative to ask.

When we become aware of requests generating costs that have not been accounted for, we need to communicate that. When we're given support tasks outside our scope or rework created by a lack of planning or site preparedness, your crew manager or project manager should be notified of these changes to our task load by you. Yes you! They should be given our estimate of the level of effort needed so they can decide where the task can be billed, make a call on its overall necessity, or even look for ways to alleviate future lack of planning and preparedness by better coordinating with the project team.

Story:

Throughout the course of my career I've worked with companies that tracked costs in all kinds of different ways, and those ways didn't always reflect dollars to the people in the field. Some of the companies used mobilizations, and some of them dictated the amount of hours you could spend on a task. I've even worked for companies that didn't express any expectations. "Just go show up" or "This is where you're going to be today.' The surveyor might just think you mean eight hours or that you want them there for as long as it takes. Unexpressed expectations of cost are dangerous because everything has an associated price. Everything has a bottom number or a top number, the breaking point between worth it and not worth it.

Budget is always something to be considered no matter our understanding of the project. In other words, we all know either our budget, our scope, or have had expectations regarding cost clearly communicated to us. In this way, when we identify something outside of scope, something with an additional level of effort or something that's been added to our plate, it triggers the conversation of cost. Not necessarily the number, that's not what I'm trying to dictate here, but rather, the need to communicate when it's understood an additional cost has arisen. It's very common to think, "I'd like to be helpful; let me get that done for you," and then down the road, someone comes back to you and says, "Why was this so expensive"?

You must be aware of budget, scope, or expectations of cost. If it hasn't been communicated, ask.

Application and Challenge:

Instead of answering those questions down the road, or saying, "I didn't intend to spend this much money," all of those conversations are had beforehand. My application and challenge—have conversations with crew managers, project managers, and superintendents when the red flag of additional cost gets raised in your mind. We know when that moment is. Sure, we may also think, " I have the green light to do this task," but is everyone aware of the cost and the level of effort? It's likely only you have those details so we want to make sure they are communicated ahead of time and clearly.

Lead the Crew

Introduction:

Like the conductor of an orchestra, the crew lead is responsible for providing clear direction, dictating the timing of tasks, and even setting the overall pace in which the crew performs. That means that your attention can no longer be centered around the success of your individual tasks alone; you must begin responsibly taking charge of others. Viewing their skill set, production and collaboration with the crew as a reflection of your leadership will help keep your team at the forefront of your attention and keep you looking for new ways and new opportunities to lead them to success. As the crew lead, you will often be responsible for balancing training opportunities against overall efficiency but remember, effective training creates efficiency.

Story:

I'm just going to go right back to the metaphor of the conductor leading the orchestra. Just imagine the conductor's up there waving his baton and his body movements are full of passion. Every movement is calculated and deliberate. If he wants a particular emotion to be depicted by the sound of the instruments, you can see that emotion on his body, even on his face. The conductor takes responsibility for everything happening, and he becomes what he wants to see happen. It is no different for a person taking charge of a crew. If you want haste and effectiveness, then you must move at a fast pace and be quick thinking in the way you lead the crew. If you want clear communication and regular feedback to be a regular feature of your crew, you must keep your communication direct and set the example in giving and asking for feedback yourself.

Lead your crew to the level at which you would feel confident putting your name on everything that they accomplish.

Application and Challenge:

When you need lightning-fast production, your pace has to be electrified first. Set the tone! Returning to the concept of the conductor, everything that happens is the result of or the responsibility of that conductor. If he was late motioning to the trombone or cymbals at the right time to crush the apex of the music, who ultimately takes the fault, the leader or the listener? In the same way with your crew, assume personal responsibility for what's happening under your care and hold the belief that your name is on the work of others as well. Once you take on a role as leader, your effort, attention, care, mentoring—each of those things has the potential to create an environment which is a true representation of your leadership.

Train Others

Introduction:

We may have a variety of experience and we may have performed certain tasks with enough repetition to know them forward and backwards. Maybe we've only got one year of experience compared to someone else's one month. In every case, share what you have learned. How did you make it faster? What obstacles are you now aware of? What was your path to success? Sure, we may not be running company-wide trainings or representing ourselves as subject matter in all things but speak up when your knowledge is helpful and relevant. Whenever we're in a position to add value to the professional abilities of others, we should take the opportunity to do just that. Improvement should always be on our minds. As our career progresses, it often becomes our role to develop other surveyors in a training capacity. If training is part of our task load, we want to make sure that training moments are our primary focus. As the budget allows, we should take every opportunity to sharpen existing skills and train on new concepts that should be a part of their future knowledge base. The order of our training can also make a big impact. We may feel that we need to deliver as much knowledge about the profession as possible as quickly as possible, but oftentimes, fully developing a concept and allowing it to take root before moving on is the most effective way to build a solid foundation for more learning. However, our training methods need to be effective if we want to create knowledge that sticks. Take time to understand the learning styles of the people you train and utilize those styles in the way you approach them. Keep information concise and to the point. Would a sketch or a 5-minute video do more to explain a particular function than an hour of explanation. Would a hands-on experience do more than a classroom environment? Time and effort spent training daily will pay for itself immediately as you help create professionals who visualize, solve, and perform tasks faster than they did the day before.

Story:

I worked with a party chief at my very first employment in the survey industry. I was running a level loop and we had radios to help us communicate. I was coming off the benchmark; it was something that I had done in technical college, but I hadn't done it out on the field before. The surveyor started to wave me over with a hand gesture, but when I started walking, he motioned for me to stop and go back. "Okay, no problem," I thought. So, I went back and put the rod on the brass cap again, and then he waved for me to come towards him again. As I started forward, he took his radio off and threw it into some nearby bushes then started walking over to me with a pissed off look on his face, very obviously cursing my existence under his breath. What he wanted to communicate to me was to "rock the rod," but I wasn't getting it because I hadn't seen the hand signals before. I didn't have the training required, I didn't possess the information necessary to complete the task the way he wanted it to be completed, and at the time, I definitely was not smart enough to just figure out what his needs were. Rather than communicating and instead of holding a quick training session, he elected to just grab the nearest object and throw it into space. If there were reunions for surveyors, I would go just to give him the "read the middle crosshair" hand signal and see if he understood it.

There is a huge difference between training and training in a way that's effective.

Application and Challenge:

We must train in a way that is effective. It is extremely common to experience training which simply checks the box of "we trained you on this," but isn't effective, memorable or delivered in a way that truly teaches. We've all been a part of a meeting that's entirely composed of a long-winded PowerPoint, and pretty soon we're trying not to get caught asleep. I teach surveying at Arizona State University, and there are times when I'm describing something mathematically that I can see the glaze just pour over people's eyes right in front of me. Are there better, more effective ways for us to teach than standing in front of people and talking "at" them? Absolutely; being ready and capable of modifying our approach to effectively reach our audience must be our primary concern. The application and challenge in this segment is one of my favorites. Applied training on this concept has been heavily featured in our boot camps. The next time someone is explaining something to you, notice the methods they use to communicate. Observing their communication style is the quickest most effective way to understand exactly how they want to be trained and communicated with.

If someone is in the middle of the learning process and they start drawing a picture or moving things around on the table to replicate the situation, you just got the clue of a lifetime. This is a visual learner who would benefit best from pictures, diagrams, and visual aids. If you drew a sketch but they want to repeat the steps vocally, or write down the instructions as you're drawing, you're witnessing their communication style. Maybe they're shaking their head while you're talking because listening is confusing them even more. Too many words! They just want to go put their hands on the equipment and see for themselves how it operates. That's exactly how they're going to learn best, and they are communicating it to you. We have to reject the desire to just teach in the method we like best or default to common training methods just because they are.. well.. common. Look for the communication styles people reveal to you and train them in the way that works best for them. Never be afraid to just ask, "How do you learn best?" and put yourself in the position to train effectively right from the start.

Becoming a Mentor

Introduction:

A mentor is a person who is invested in the long-term development of others. The sincere desire to see another individual succeed creates the attention and effort needed to stand back and observe a person's weaknesses and strengths, to create dependable and timely feedback (whether commendation or feedback for improvement). As a mentor, our own ability to be vulnerable about our mistakes and missteps creates a person-to-person bond that is bigger than our professional development alone. Our genuine feedback doesn't need to be just technical in nature. Soft skills, such as how they communicate and controlling or applying their emotional range to situations at the appropriate time, may be the type of personal development that brings lasting impact on the career, personal life, and day-to-day happiness of those we mentor. Do you remember the mentors over the course of your career? How often did they weigh in on concepts over and above technical skills?

Story:

In my own recent training/mentoring history. I had the opportunity to talk with someone regarding the way they wrote emails and give feedback for improvement. They would write emails which were technically sound that stated the facts just as they were, but in reading them as someone outside of the situation, I could see how they might be interpreted as defensive, maybe even uncaring or inconsiderate towards what the project team was experiencing on the jobsite. They just sounded rude and disconnected. So, we talked about using different words and phrases that communicated he understood the importance of what they had to say and that he would come up with an action plan, so they didn't have a similar experience in the future. The truth was he did care, but without stating that, the project team couldn't tell. Moving forward, as he proofread his messages, he would ask himself, "Do the words in my email help them feel better about the situation or do I sound personally detached?" Yes, there are tons of technical skills we can teach, but when we're a mentor, the focus is different. Some of the key words are "invested" and "person-to-person." A mentor is not just a trainer. The mindset of a mentor is truly sincere, "I'm deeply concerned about your growth, and I want to do everything I can to help you succeed." Not, "Hey, here's a little bit of technical data to infer in a while." Mentoring is much more focused on the well-rounded development of the entire person. We don't have to pigeon-hole or focus our mentoring or teaching ability to just the technical aspect or just the money-making skills. The focus is their career, their development as a professional, and fulfillment as a human being— results that will show up in the ways they deal with people, the speed in which they get irritated or take things in stride, the way they answer a text message, even the way they make people feel when they show up on a jobsite. All those things drive their professional experience, and if we're truly invested and take the time to create a solid relationship, we'll feel comfortable weighing in on all those areas of development.

Focus on the development of the whole person. This creates true investment and a sincere bond between mentor and mentee.

Application and Challenge:

If you're a person who's in the mentoring position, ask yourself how often you're weighing in outside of technical abilities. Look for more opportunities to sincerely affect the people you mentor professionally as they move forward in their career and in the experiences that make up their lives.

Weigh-in on Costs and Participate in Bidding

Introduction:

Whether you're the boots on the ground looking to better understand your project's overall budget or learning to determine task and project cost in a way that makes you competitive and relevant to your market, get in there. Vocalize your thought process in determining task hours or project cost and become part of the conversation. Get feedback based on the experience of others and create intelligent metrics that allow you to gauge cost effectively with the least amount of time spent. If you have access to budget spreadsheets, take one home. Study what you see against the plan set. Find out what assumptions are being made regarding your scope or how things are most commonly done in the industry. Ask for a blank spreadsheet, bid your own tasks or jobs, and compare with the figures created by management. Don't be afraid to ask questions. The application of experience is huge in determining cost so the sooner you start to exercise your experience in this area, the faster you'll be creating intelligent and accurate bids of your own.

Story:

Getting started in costs and bidding has turned into a major facet of my task load as a manager. At the outset, I was always surprised how quickly costs multiplied. Things that seemed relatively simple or inexpensive in my mind took on cost and became something expensive. I've worked on projects as small as boundary surveys for single-family homes, and even those things can run up a price tag quickly. Recognizing the difference between what I thought and where costs were is what drove me to dig deeper and begin learning "why." I started to bid on the projects I was working on or on tasks such as laying out the sewer or on-site curb just to see how my ideas of duration and value compared with costs determined by the experts. If I saw a big disparity between what I thought versus reality, I'd ask questions to determine what I was missing or what I was failing to visualize when I thought about the overall task.

Find out the how and why behind project costs.

Application and Challenge:

Visualizing cost will help us be cost-effective while we're boots on the ground, on-site. It will also help us win projects from a bidding standpoint and avoid coming in with a cost that's way too low and doesn't represent the work being done. A bid created without true understanding of cost can leave us on the hook to be underpaid for something more involved and more expensive than anyone took into consideration. Start bidding individual tasks or entire projects and compare notes with the experts. Ask for feedback. Find out the "why" when you see major differences. The sooner you get involved, the sooner you'll be putting together comprehensive bids that are utilized by the project team and lead to profit and departmental success.

Determining Your Sweet Spot

Introduction:

Do what you're damn good at. Make a name for yourself. Is there something you do the fastest or the most accurately? Is there something that comes naturally to you or that you've worked at perfecting? Find your sweet spot within the company. As a company, find your sweet spot within the industry. You can find it by measuring performance. You can carve out your sweet spot because you know exactly what you want to do. You may even determine a specific need in the industry and rise to meet it. We should never stop growing or accumulating new experiences. There is always room for technical and professional development. The key is to ask yourself if you are busy doing what keeps you the most satisfied, the most challenged, and the most financially rewarded. Are you using the skill set that makes you the most valuable to the company? The sweet spot is not a place to "rest" on what you already know; it's the place that uncovers your most valuable self by utilizing your greatest potential.

Story:

I'd like to give an example of how to end up in your sweet spot. I'll give you some details of how I arrived at managing and mentoring surveyors in multiple states, moderating boot camps, traveling the country as a consultant, and teaching Construction Surveying at Arizona State University. To be honest, all these things began in pretty close conjunction with each other, all circulating around me as I pursued my sweet spot. I had the opportunity to work with Jason as a mentor for field engineers at my first boot camp. I really liked what was going on. I resonated with the culture being promoted and the focus on personal development as the shuttle for professional development. I felt there were things I had put into practice from my own professional development training at the Rapport School of Leadership (which I strongly recommend to anyone ready to take their own development to the next level). I knew there were things I could bring more directly to the boot camp outside of just technical expertise. I took the initiative and used my platform to speak up about them. I hadn't been asked to do so, but I wanted to assist in the growth taking place in every way I could. Once I put myself out there, taking the initiative to declare what was important to me, I showed up on Jason's radar. This is not to say he didn't appreciate me before, but now he had a deeper understanding of what was important to me and what I could offer. There were even a few times he asked me, "Hey, what do you think I could do better? How do you think this is going?" Once I had put myself out there to be understood by him, Jason started making more opportunities for me to share my philosophies, and I took the initiative to share as much as I could.

I couldn't have been happier than watching people blossom in their careers and personal lives, so at one point I just took Jason aside and said "Hey, I would like to do this with you in the future; whatever you're gonna do, take me with you." Some people may view this as a self-embarrassing statement similar to "I'd like to stick to you like a sucker fish and basically follow you around," but hey, that is what I wanted to do! I wanted to keep doing boot camps, I wanted to associate with people I felt were motivating and had a clear goal in life, people who made it their purpose to build up others around them. Why would I let my ego stand in the way of defining my own purpose? So yes, I said "Hey, take me with you!" As a result, my position at Okland changed from one that had been strictly geared towards survey and technical training to overall professional development for field engineers, putting together trainings for superintendents, and later, a permanent role consulting with Elevate. Yes, I had to ignore my ego. Yes, I had to have tough conversations to get what I wanted. No, it wasn't easy. Yes, it meant much more effort at the everyday level. But I've proven to myself it is possible to determine exactly what you enjoy or what truly satisfies you, and to simply go and chase that down until you catch it.

Do what you're damn good at!

Application and Challenge:

Have you identified what it is that makes you feel satisfied in your career, and have you thought about how you could capitalize on, focus, or enhance that component of your career? Have you put your ideas out there to see if you could enhance the value of your company in performing that specific role? Here's an example: Maybe you're excellent at doing topographic surveys and you will likely be the person who performs all the high-profile detailed surveys. But... could you instead be the person who teaches everyone at your company to do topographic surveys or how to shoot points in the way the drafting tech needs. Maybe you could do little demos out in the field or provide best practice examples of sketches and notes for training. A small training role slowly evolves into department-wide training and procedure development. You're watching crews evolve, you're experiencing the camaraderie you love, and you can say, "Man, I'm really living what I like to do." There are so many ways to get moving down the path to living your sweet spot. First, identify it. What would it look like to you? If you can't see the detail in how it might enhance your career or your company, the second step is talking to your department manager about it. "Hey, I'm the best at this. What can I do to benefit the company in a bigger way with this knowledge or these skills?" Get your ideas out there and see what they have to say. Between your two schools of thought, you may really find that it's not that hard to end up doing what you love and what deeply satisfies you.

Interpreting/Writing Scopes and Verbiage

Introduction:

The devil is in the details. An intelligently written scope uses detailed verbiage to ensure what you intended and how you intended it comes to pass. Here's an example: Sanitary sewer layout, all structures, bends and a maximum of 30' intervals along SS alignments. Task Cost: $XXXX.XX What if the superintendent breaks this up into 4 mobilizations and it could have been accomplished in 2 with adequate planning. What if the contractor asks for stakes on center along with both 10- and 15-foot offsets, effectively tripling your staking work? Take the time to consider how your intention will take place when you write out a general scope item and add those details to your verbiage. Sanitary sewer layout, 2 mobilizations maximum. 2 offset stakes set at each structure and bend; 1 offset stake set at a 30' interval maximum along SS alignments. Task Cost: $XXXX.XX Additional mobilizations to be charged at 2-person crew hourly rate. See rate table. Clearly describing your expectation is the best way to ensure your expectation is met.

Story:

I worked for a company that utilized mobilizations and they held to their contract mobilizations from a cost standpoint more than they did the specific task. In their contract verbiage it defined how mobilizations were computed, assuming a minimum amount of work could be done on each visit. Not only did it force the project team to think ahead and ensure site readiness, but it ensured the project team was utilizing both survey and its budget efficiently. As you read their verbiage, you didn't even want an overall task cost, you wanted to see the project team plan mobilizations and be effective. Once those mobilizations were exceeded, it was clear to everyone additional costs were being generated and in almost every case, it forced the project team to consider their planning more efficiently moving forward.

When you think about additional work and change orders—yes, that's a safety net for you—but it could be a negative to your relationship with the project team, client, or owner. The point of this section isn't to get every penny you can but instead, to make sure that we're considering and communicating our intentions clearly. In this way, if things do go wrong, everyone understands why and how it will be addressed moving forward. No surprises. Nothing can injure a strong business relationship like squabbling over recollections, conversations, and the dreaded "I thought..." Conversely, when something is written down plain as day on a sheet of paper and everyone can look back at it and say this is what happened, this is avoided. It's much simpler to maintain expectations and allow you to solidify your relationships even when things don't go as planned. When expectations are clear, everyone knows the goal they're working towards. Those goals are more likely to be met completely in the long run and everyone is on the same page from a cost standpoint.

Clear expectations create a clearly defined path to success.

Application and Challenge:

If you're a crew manager or a department manager, take a look at the verbiage that has been put together to represent your work. Maybe it's being put together by someone else entirely. Your scope and budget verbiage may have been created by business development, a bidding team, or finance. Make sure the verbiage accurately represents what you intend and practice going through it from the standpoint of an outsider to ensure it can't be misinterpreted. Remember, there's nothing wrong with being overly specific in communicating those intentions. Using things like mobilizations, specifying the amount of stakes, defining the amount of trips, or explaining cost if overages occur means there will be absolutely no surprises for you or your future business relationships.

Managing Multiple Teams

Introduction:

As you move into management—whether you're managing multiple people in a crew, multiple crews on a site, or a department as a whole—ask yourself if you would still put your name on the work being accomplished. If not, what would it take to get your buy-in? Check in regularly, find out what methods are being used on-site, listen to the planned approach created by your team leads, and listen to their estimates for time. Make site visits to observe how the team performs work and collaborates with the rest of the project team. Like a watch, all parts should be working together and in sync with one another. Take time to step back and observe the function of each person, each component. Provide feedback for improvement and follow through to the application of that feedback. Train and appoint leads who can be trusted to hold the line to the same degree you would when it comes to quality. Only when you're comfortable putting your name on the deliverables and work in place created under your supervision can you truly say, "I have successfully managed this team."

Story:

During my early days at the walkie-talkie throwing company, all the party chiefs did things completely different according to what they felt was best. If a party chief was asked to perform work on someone else's project, he had a difficult time picking up where that person left off or interfacing with the project team in the same way because they were all using such different methods and schools of thought. Our clients grew used to certain people and wanted them back on the job, sometimes to the point of firing the current surveyor from the project. Why do you think our end product was such a mixed bag? When there is no "lead" getting out in the field to look at, review, and direct how work is done, how will the crews ever have a true north regarding their work? There must be someone to define what is best assisting the crews to constantly hit that mark.

We all appreciate independence and individuality. There can be plenty of different ways to accomplish a particular task and individually, we may have been trained in different ways. But if there's a best way, shouldn't we all be doing it? In the introduction, we talked about training and appointing leads who can be trusted to hold the line to the same degree as we hold ourselves. From a crew manager's standpoint, you have to be in front of those teams providing feedback for improvement, additional training, or whatever is necessary. When you can't be there, you should have the peace of mind that the leads you have appointed think the way you do or would perform the way you do so your name could be on that work.

If there's a best way, shouldn't we all be doing it?

Application and Challenge:

Right now, would you put your name on the work of each person on your crews? I bet you wouldn't. Let's admit it's sad to say, but at the same time in our minds we're saying, "I just don't have the bandwidth to be there at that level." Can we work more closely with the person who does have the bandwidth? Can we create a position for a person with the bandwidth? What needs to happen so that theoretically, every stake, every nail, every painted target, and every drafted exhibit left behind as a product would have our name on it. What would it take?

Managing Multiple Clients, Multiple Trades

Introduction:

Build rapport with your clients and trade partners. Your aim should be learning how to work hand-in-hand with them in the most effective way as a team. This means listening closely to their needs and uncovering their communication styles. Help them vocalize their expectations. Likewise, your clients and trade partners should be able to rely on you to communicate clearly, declare your expectations and intentions, merge that vision with theirs, and hold yourself accountable. The beauty of accountability is that it is a two-way street. As people see you hold yourself accountable to your word and your actions, they will rise to meet you at that level. This creates an environment in which you can hold each other accountable to perform in accord with your stated agreements. You, just like managing crews, need to visit the site. Get to know faces and stay in touch with site progress. This first-hand knowledge will assist you in communicating realistic timelines and obtaining flexibility and cooperation when needed.

Story:

The following story takes place in the great state of Texas where they have breakfast tacos, not breakfast burritos. If you use the term "breakfast burritos," it's the same as admitting you're from another planet or were raised by wolves. There was a project manager at a company I worked for who would take breakfast tacos to the jobsites to shake hands and have quick conversations with the PMs and superintendents before making his way back to the office. He was literally loved, number one, because breakfast tacos really are that good, but it also put a face to the person they were regularly communicating with, and they ultimately felt a kinship to that person. At the beginning of the introduction in this section, it says "build rapport." A little lower down, the print reads "firsthand knowledge" and "visit the site." We're describing sincere connection, aren't we? Whether you're managing crews, clients, or trades, you must be present and you must establish genuine connection. You're not going to accomplish these things through emails and text messages alone (although they can be avenues you use to maintain relationships). The ability to connect sincerely must come from your desire to see others be successful and happy and to actively recognize your ability to affect that outcome.

When you're connected in that way, it is so much easier to be remarkably clear and direct with somebody. Communication comes easier, more often. They know you have good intentions; they've met you, they'll be able to take it as a benefit when you're direct with them, and they'll feel comfortable doing the same thing from a place of honesty and mutual accountability. They will even view you as a better friend when you hold them accountable because it will signal you have faith in their ability to be the best version of themselves and will help push them to do so. These kinds of relationships take time to create and maintain, but that effort is tied to just how effective we can be.

Rapport: (noun) A close and harmonious relationship in which the people or groups concerned understand each other's feelings or ideas and communicate well.

Application and Challenge:

Do you know the faces of the clients you manage? Have you talked to the foremen of the trades that you're working closely with or preparing information for? It can go such a long way to meet those people, even once. Some companies have niceties delivered like donuts or snacks, but visiting people where they work, as they work, and seeing the site—those things go so much further than a congenial relationship. Only when the boots on the ground see our boots out there in the mud with them will they believe we can understand their needs and their struggles.

Bonus Story:

On one of my earlier jobs in the Phoenix area, I was working with a trade partner and their draftsperson trying to align our CAD models for some tight tolerance layout needs. We were using civil coordinates and survey control, and they were coming from shop drawings that were basically in a zero-zero coordinate world. They were having a hard time reconciling data, getting onto our coordinate system, and enabling their layout technician to start working more independently. I elected to make my way out to the jobsite and sit in their trailer with their drafting technician to compare our data. I taught him how to translate/rotate line work in AutoCAD and then QC coordinates to ensure we were in the right spot. I was probably there for the first half of the day. After that, I was friends with everyone in that trailer. Anytime I saw any of those guys on any site in the future—their layout technician or their drafting guy—I could see their eyes light up with a big smile because they saw me, and they recognized "This is a person who wants to see me succeed!" What a great way to feel about other people, and it's a great way to be viewed. There are so many little extra mile things we could do to interface with our clients and trades to empower them to be successful. Which ones are you going to put into effect?

Build a Cohesive Department

Introduction:

In a cohesive world, everyone works and sticks together. There are no silos in which one person or group separates themselves and loses connection and communication with the overall team. When silos exist there is often miscommunication, duplicated work, similar efforts headed in opposing directions, competition versus collaboration, resentment, mixed signals to our clients and trade partners, and a slew of poor departmental behaviors. Sometimes, when we meet opposition to our ideas, we choose to distance ourselves from that perceived threat. Other times, when our team feels opposition from within, they will push that person out of the group. In either scenario, a silo has been created and the team can no longer prosper as a whole. They will never achieve the success they would as a cohesive department.

Story:

In our boot camps, we have a team activity that simulates a complex scenario for participants. As things get tough, one of the first things we typically see happen is a whole bunch of silos being created. The introverts turn into a silo of one. They sometimes go into their heads, start thinking, but stop communicating. There are silo groups of two or three who are already comfortable communicating with each other, but no one else. Often the extroverts are speaking over the others, and some people disconnect and shut down because, well, someone has taken the reins and they are no longer needed. Communication deteriorates at an alarming rate and in that siloed structure, nothing happens. There's no movement forward. If anything, the many independent groups begin creating movements in opposite directions, re-working the same ideas over and over. How does your department react under pressure?

A cohesive department is one that actively maintains communication through stress, opposition, and heavy workload.

Application and Challenge:

When we meet opposition, people tend to distance themselves—creating a silo effect. When a team feels opposition, they might push someone out of the group and silo that person's efforts and ideas. Is that something you ever find yourself becoming involved in? Or is your go-to distancing yourself and retreating into the comfort of your own thoughts when times get tough? It's pretty common to observe that kind of behavior in the workplace, and you're not being shunned here if you identify with the above. You're simply receiving the information that there's a better environment available, and the path to creating it is to keep communication clear, direct, and plentiful. In this way, the individual team and the greater department knows what the plan is, what the specifics are, who's doing what, and none of the debilitating breakdowns in communication have an opportunity to take root.

Create a Culture

Introduction:

Determine your values, declare them, and act on them. If your value is quality, every individual within the department should be working at quality, thinking quality, and brainstorming new ways to achieve quality. A culture isn't just words, it's a way of being. Meaning those managing the team need to be the example of the culture in every interaction. They must look for ways to weave the culture into each task, each deliverable, each client experience. A culture of accountability is unstoppable. When you know you'll be held responsible for the quality of your product, what level of attention will you bring? When you know everyone else is committed to their best, how will you choose to perform? Normalize the vocalization of expectations and intentions. Normalize commendation when it's sincere and feedback for improvement when it's needed. Create buy-in for holding each other accountable so that each member of the team knows they are supported by people who truly believe in them. Be the culture you want to see everywhere you go. Don't allow yourself to be sucked into the cultures of negativity, blaming, and half efforts that surround us everywhere we look.

Story:

So, my personal culture—okay, it sounds really funny to say "my personal culture" because culture sounds like something that's taken on by people—is that I stand for quality. I like to make things in my down time. I refinish furniture and I make ornate picture frames. There are a whole bunch of different crafts that I do, and they take so long to finish. It's not related to effort or cost; it's about making something that's so damn beautiful when I'm done every time, I look at it, I tell myself, "This is beautiful." I did what I set out to do and I didn't compromise. That makes me so happy.

Also, as a person, it's part of my culture to help other people grow. It's become part of my work with Okland, it's the focus of my consulting with Elevate, and it is part of how I interface with everybody in my life, literally. It doesn't matter who you are, if you interact with me, that will be a part of the takeaway. That's what I want to see in my life, so that's how I act. When I find others who are of my culture, I attach myself to them. I push for company initiatives that help foster culture, and I work to be an example of that culture to lead the way. Those are the things in my culture.

How do you survey perfectly when there are tasks another company will do for half the cost with a GPS unit, BOOM! and slap it in the ground? Well, Okland is a company that wants to turn out quality, one-of-a-kind products and experiences. In that way, we align heavily. Through communication, I worked with them to determine a sweet spot based on that culture and quality. Our survey department focuses on things only we can do best from a quality standpoint, and tasks that don't require that level of attention are bid out to the "BOOM! slap it in the ground" company. We stay true to culture and keep costs low at the same time. When culture is related to your own personal buy-in, it becomes easy to sustain and pour effort into every day.

Be the environment you want to see around you.

Application and Challenge:

Have you ever walked into a job shack—maybe it's even your own company's trailer—and everybody just looks up at you for a second then looks back down at their work? No

150

hellos, no smiles. You feel as unimportant and invisible as a draft blowing the door open for a second, which is about as much notice or care anyone has about you. The culture in that trailer feels negative and makes you sad just to be there. Nope, sorry everybody. I don't care. I don't care that you wanted to be expressionless and unexcitable about life. I am the environment, and my culture is to help people and make them feel better. When I walk into that dreary old trailer and trip over that couldn't-care-less attitude, it's immediately time for me to start greeting people, "Hey, how are you!? How's that going, how's this going? How's your son? When's your next family trip? Have we been supporting you well enough? What could I do better?" I just have to start asking questions from a place of sincerity and be the culture I want to see wherever I go. I do feel like my department is made up of quality people who want to help others—and that makes me so proud to be a part of it—but I can't wait for them to create the environment for me. When I walk into a cultureless Drearysville, I'm going to bring them one so they can feel happy and successful and known—just like I want to! My challenge is for you to "be the environment you want to see around you," especially when you experience the opposite. Buy-in, hunker down, and settle deep into being that environment always. Push your culture, especially where you feel adversity to it.

(From Jason) I usually don't comment "cause hey, this book is going beautifully," but in his book, *Extreme Ownership*, by Jocko Willink constantly said, "It's your fault. You need to do it. You always have to." When you first read those words, they can seem a little bit like, "Whoa, that's pretty off-putting." This is the magic secret sauce to anything on Earth. If you want to create a culture, be that culture. If you want a clean job, be clean. If you want to have a great family, be a good leader in that family. Everything *is* our fault. If you want something, you have enough mental capacity, energy, and

THE ART OF THE BUILDER

will to make it happen, period. That's it, period. Just be that environment and that environment will spread. I had a conversation comparing culture to tuning forks. If you vibrate one, whichever other fork it touches will vibrate in the same way. We're tuning forks too. The energy we have will permeate throughout literally everything that we do. I couldn't agree more with what Willink said.

This doesn't mean that every single person who exists will buy into your culture just because you're so great at projecting it. There are crusty, unhappy people. There are superintendents set in their ways, and that's the way they're going to retire. There are PMs with a cynical attitude of money over culture. There are all kinds of reasons why you might experience a small percentage of people who never go along with positive culture. You will not change everybody. Instead, you will grow firmly into your culture, and no one will change you because you are relentless in the way you apply it. You won't even be discouraged by that 10% or 20% who aren't getting the message, you won't tone down your shine, you'll keep going at full force, and your culture will thrive.

How a General Contractor Can Work Effectively with the Surveyors

Introduction:

The general contractor and superintendent should be comfortable asking for constant communication including an up-to-date control plan, expectations on delivery, and a look ahead in availability when planning. They should hold the surveyor accountable to check-in and check-out daily with a plan and progress updates. When open communication hasn't been established, the project team will often make decisions and create timetables independent of the input, expertise, and awareness of potential obstacles to the surveyor's work or site production as a whole. The project team should also keep in mind even though the surveyor can accomplish a variety of tasks fairly quickly, they should aim to use them where they are the most effective and most valuable. Is the surveyor dipping into carpentry tasks or trade partner layout? Is the surveyor's total station being used as a quick QC tool over and over? Carpenters, field engineers, and trade partners should be held accountable to produce in a timely manner and perform the appropriate QC for their own tasks—whether it's with a tape and speed square, theodolite, or their own layout equipment. This frees the surveyor to stay focused on the precision activities that generate the most value for his time, attack scopes efficiently, and stay within budget.

Story:

Just writing about combining our efforts made me think more about project teams working together with a surveyor to create a control plan. This is a perfect example of what's being explained in this paragraph. Is anyone the sole owner of the knowledge of everything that will happen on the site? Of course not. The surveyor knows the things happening in their scope and in line with their technical expertise better than the superintendent does. The superintendent has knowledge of the site a surveyor doesn't possess such as where the other trade partners may be storing their equipment and construction materials. The trade partners may have ideas of when deliveries are coming related to their materials. Communication is everything. It brings all this knowledge together. If the surveyor goes to the project team and says, "I'm thinking about putting control here, here, and here," the project team pulls out their logistics plan and can see there's a conflict with the control conversation. They communicate. "This is going to get wiped out. We're staging equipment over there. There's going to be a crane here. I'm glad we're discussing this." Communicating is simply the best practice for working together. As the surveyor, you should expect that the project team is talking to you regularly. You should expect to be giving feedback to the superintendent and getting feedback from the superintendent. You can create opportunities to say, "I noticed this is happening with the site" or "I know that we won't be available until this time" or "It looks like you're ready for this other area. What's going on with that?" And you GCs and supers...you should feel comfortable holding the surveyor accountable to do all of the above, to communicate with you this way. If you're working with a surveyor who shows up on site, says nothing to you, does what's on their work order and leaves, their mindset is about checking the box of a work order. That's it. They either aren't interested or empowered to ensure your project site thrives, and their mindset needs to be changed. They need to be plugged into your project as soon as they step foot on it. This is true professionalism, and from a professional standpoint, we want to hold our surveyors accountable to what we know they can deliver.

That goes pretty deep though. It means back at that surveyor's home company, the crew lead or department manager needs to be promoting the same mindset of "Hey, we constantly communicate." What does that look like from a mentoring standpoint? The crew manager and survey department manager meet people on the site, have conversations with superintendents, and set an example on those things. We're at the start of an industry opportunity to work together and make each other better, to optimize the way we progress together, and third parties will take sincere effort and genuine interest in shared success from both sides.

Accountability is professionalism at the highest level and professionalism is shared respect.

Application and Challenge:

A consistent thread throughout this whole book is your career will be so much better if you care about it. Truly care. This takes me right back to asking, "What would you put your name on?" Do you care about the amount of communication you have with a particular person or team? Do you care about how their project turns out? Do you care about the budget and its relation to our ideas of success? Do you care how your work looks, your handwriting, and how plumb your laths are or whether they're going to get run over? When you care, you speak up and communicate for success. You won't just check the box that says, "I showed up to work and I did my activity. I did it for the right amount of hours, and I got paid," right?

We don't have to be all in but if we're not, we won't progress in our careers at a rapid pace, we won't build sincere relationships, and we won't make a profit at the same level as we would if we cared about what we did—if we were willing to put our name on all those things. As a surveyor, I care about the work I do. I care about what goes in the ground. I don't want to say "I'm afraid" but I do everything in my power to make sure nothing I write—no mistake—comes back to haunt me I want every nail to be placed in a spot where it's going to be maintained because skipping out on that effort means missed or lost production for somebody else. I care. That colors the way I do everything.

If you don't feel it already, find ways to build investment and personal buy-in for everything you do. Set yourself up to care. Work at it. In doing so, you can develop your career, a life, and a legacy you are extremely proud of!

Project Implementation Steps

Below is a list of implementation steps you can use when you approach a project as a surveyor.

Survey:

Constructability Review of All Civil Drawings:

- Basis of bearings or basis of coordinates are obtained and verified
- Design benchmark is listed with proper elevation
- Property lines shown with dimensions to building or site components
- Grid lines or building shown with coordinates or dimensions from the property line so building can be located spatially

Grid lines dimensions reviewed for accuracy and agreement sheet to sheetCAD Interface - Setup Base Files:

- Obtain CAD drawing files for existing conditions and civil design
- Confirm basis of coordinates
- Confirm synchrony of line work from CAD to plan set
- Overlay drawings and create staking/working base file
- Request civil coordinates for grid line placement from Civil/Architect
- Draw all project grid lines and double-check against plan dimensions
- Circulate base for use inter-department or in field

Procure and Contract Professional Surveyors (when applicable):

- Create detailed inclusion of survey requirements at project start-up

- Get multiple estimates and review assumptions in scope to compare

- Select surveyor and coordinate future work

- Ensure coordination between survey and project team regarding location and protection of project control

Setup Primary Control:

- Reference basis of bearings or basis of coordinates

- Establish permanent control such as brass monuments or concrete monuments for longevity when possible

- Traverse points and fine tune to better than 0.015' tolerance

- Run closed level loop through all points and adjust

- Provide certified control drawing showing all points with XYZ values adjusted to project/task tolerance

- Coordinate adjusted control with all involved parties and trades

- Provide field notes for all survey work

- Field label all adjusted control and protect

- Create base CAD file or point file for distribution

Establish Secondary Control (Building grid lines):

- Plan offsets and placement location for grid line staking with project team

- Establish secondary control by shooting base line ends from a minimum of 3 points and averaging

- Shoot intermediate points along line establishing a baseline with a minimum of 4 points along the long side of the building

- Turn averaged 90s, double verify distances and establish short sides of building (as requested)

- Close secondary control figure and check square (as requested)

- As-built adjacent existing buildings and structures and RFI if locations are out of design tolerance with new building

- Confirm no inaccuracies or errors in measurement are included in your building placement

- Correct deficiencies as necessary

General Survey
Startup Tasks for Construction

The list below may be helpful to project teams as they consider help needed from a surveyor.

1. Confirm schedule dates on 90-day startup schedule
2. Review the site utilization plan
3. Order equipment to meet project needs for field engineers
4. Request CAD drawings from Civil and Survey
5. Compile base drawing files
6. Create site control plan with input from project team and site logistics
7. Establish primary control with survey and field engineers
8. Pothole tentative utility crossings to verify placement
9. Locate utilities, as-builts, BlueStake or any other information to verify existing condition data
10. Update site utility map for planning and excavation
11. Establish secondary control with field engineers
12. Begin calculating layout, task planning as requested

Survey Tool Belt Setup Recommendations

Below is a list of recommended tools as a professional surveyor.

1. Snap together tool belt (faster on/off and they last years)

2. Phone in belt holder with ringer ON (so you don't miss calls)

3. Inches and tenths engineer's tape measure (to QC both units in the field)

4. 32 oz. smooth-faced hammer (doesn't eat up hubs or lath, heavy enough for rebar)

5. Easy deployment hammer holder

6. Round tip, serrated knife (cutting, sawing, clearing branches, round tip let's you widdle written mistakes off of lath)

7. Wire cutting/tying pliers

8. Accessory ring with carabiners for attaching high-use quick release items

9. Tack ball with hub tacks (enough tacks for task, replaced regularly)

10. Small whisk broom (clean/clear working surfaces, prep for stickers. You'll use it every day if you keep it handy)

11. Multi-tool (I like the Leatherman Wave. It has needle nose pliers, solid screwdrivers, round tip blade for lath, saw and file)

12. Paint can holder with accessory/marker slots (always have pink paint for highlighting, swap with clear-coat depending on work)

13. Extra marker

14. Railroad spike to prehammer tough ground for hub and lath (carrying the lightest/smallest option means you always have it with you)

15. Extra pouch- filled with pink feathered 60-D nails when staking

16. Plumb bob replaces 60-D nails when performing building layout (peanut prism with plumb bob string C-mount always sitting in breast pocket)

Surveyor Daily Tasks

Below is a list of recommended tasks to perform daily.

- Check-in with the office team about plan for the day
- Check-in with the project team before starting
- Actively prepare your work environment before leaving and on-site
- Perform all double-checks
- Review your work in the field with the on-site team before leaving
- Review your notes and field work in the office

Surveyor Secret Sauce

Below is a list of secret sauce items that really make a good surveyor.

- Punctual
- Always double-checks the work
- Well-rounded tool bag and always has the tools with them
- Cares for equipment. Clean, assess and calibrate regularly
- Always checks in with the project team to start and before leaving
- Is approachable
- Communicates well, thinks collaboratively
- Is professional
- Goes the extra mile
- Takes care of the customer, not just the work order
- Doesn't get angry
- Is always improving knowledge base
- Understands building construction
- Is honest and direct
- Doesn't hide errors

Conclusion

This is your career. You are right in the middle of the decisions you have made which will shape your path, your success and ultimately, your happiness. It's our desire that this text motivates you to pursue and take hold of exactly what you want from life, from the small things to the large. Your career will define one of the largest requirements of time and attention you will experience in this short life. There's no reason to spend your experience working in a field that doesn't make you happy or in an environment that breeds negativity. You are at the center of every choice and every action. You are at the center of every emotion felt along the way. You are the creator of this experience.

Determine your culture and stick to the people who support your journey. There is no time for comfort or apathy. Keep moving forward.

On we go!
Brandon & Jason

P.S.

This book is a draft edition! We are publishing it to garner feedback, stories, and corrections from the industry we love and respect. There are so many professionals with stories, experiences, and wisdom that should be shared in the official publishing of this book. You are likely one of these. If so, we are asking for your feedback and contributions. Please send it to jasons@elevateconstructionist.com and we will add you to the list of contributors.

THE END

Remember, perfection is the new standard!

Made in the USA
Middletown, DE
05 April 2023

28327015R00102